LEISURE ARTS PRESENTS

Christmas Portraits

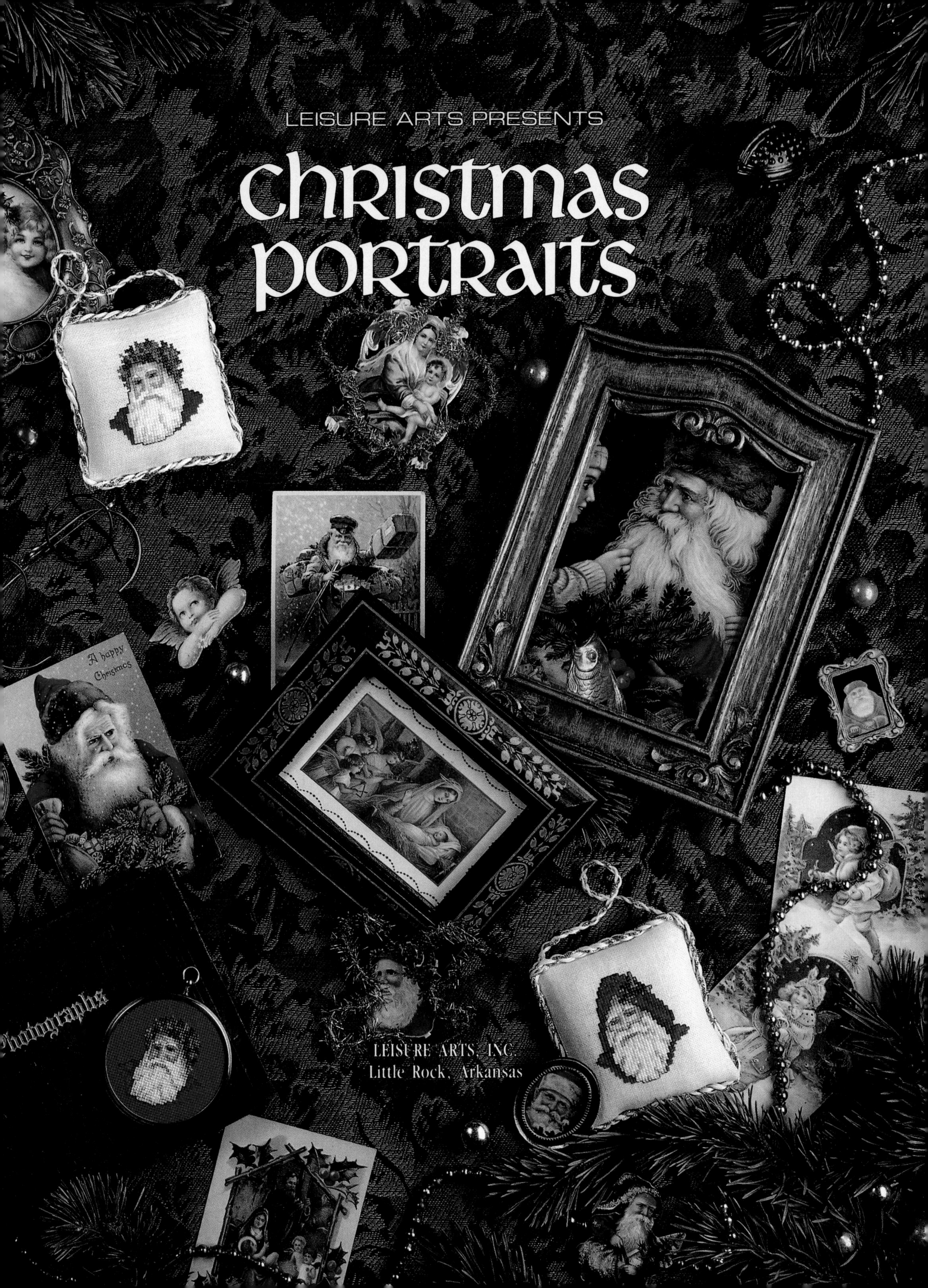

LEISURE ARTS, INC.
Little Rock, Arkansas

EDITORIAL STAFF

Editor: Anne Van Wagner Childs. *Executive Director:* Sandra Graham Case. *Creative Art Director:* Gloria Bearden *Executive Editor:* Susan Frantz Wiles. PRODUCTION — *Managing Editor:* Carla Bentley. *Senior Editor:* Susan Sullivan. *Project Coordinator:* Pam Young. EDITORIAL — *Associate Editor:* Dorothy Latimer Johnson. *Senior Editorial Writer:* Tammi Williamson-Bradley. *Editorial Writers:* Marjorie Lacy Bishop and Holly Leigh Sel *Editorial Copy Assistants:* Laurie R. Burleson, Darla Burdette Kelsay, and Linda L. Trimble. *Advertising and Direct Mail Senior Copywriter:* Eva M. Delfos. ART — *Production Art Director:* Melinda Stout. *Senior Production Artist:* Linda Lovette. *Chart Production Artist:* Cindy Zimmerebner. *Photography Stylist:* Karen Smart Hal *Typesetters:* Cindy Lumpkin and Stephanie Cordero. *Advertising and Direct Mail Artists:* Sondra Harrison Dani and Kathleen Murphy.

BUSINESS STAFF

Publisher: Steve Patterson. *Controller:* Tom Siebenmorgen. *Retail Sales Director:* Richard Tignor. *Retail Marketing Director:* Pam Stebbins. *Retail Customer Services Director:* Margaret Sweetin. *Marketing Manager:* Russ Barnet *Executive Director of Marketing and Circulation:* Guy A. Crossley. *Fulfillment Manager:* Scott Sharpe. *Print Production:* Nancy Reddick Lister and Laura Lockhart.

CREDITS

NEEDLEWORK ADAPTATIONS: We offer our sincere thank you to Carol Emmer, whose wonderful needlewor adaptations have once again helped create a book of beautiful Christmas cross stitch. A special word of thank is also given to Jane Chandler for her additional needlework adaptations. PHOTOGRAPHY: Ken West, Larr Pennington, and Mark Mathews of Peerless Photography, Little Rock, Arkansas. COLOR SEPARATIONS: Magn IV Engravers of Little Rock, Arkansas. PHOTO ACCESSORIES: Chambers Drug Store and Country Treasure of Jacksonville, Arkansas, porcelain dolls, pages 6-7.

International Standard Book Number 0-942237-12-9

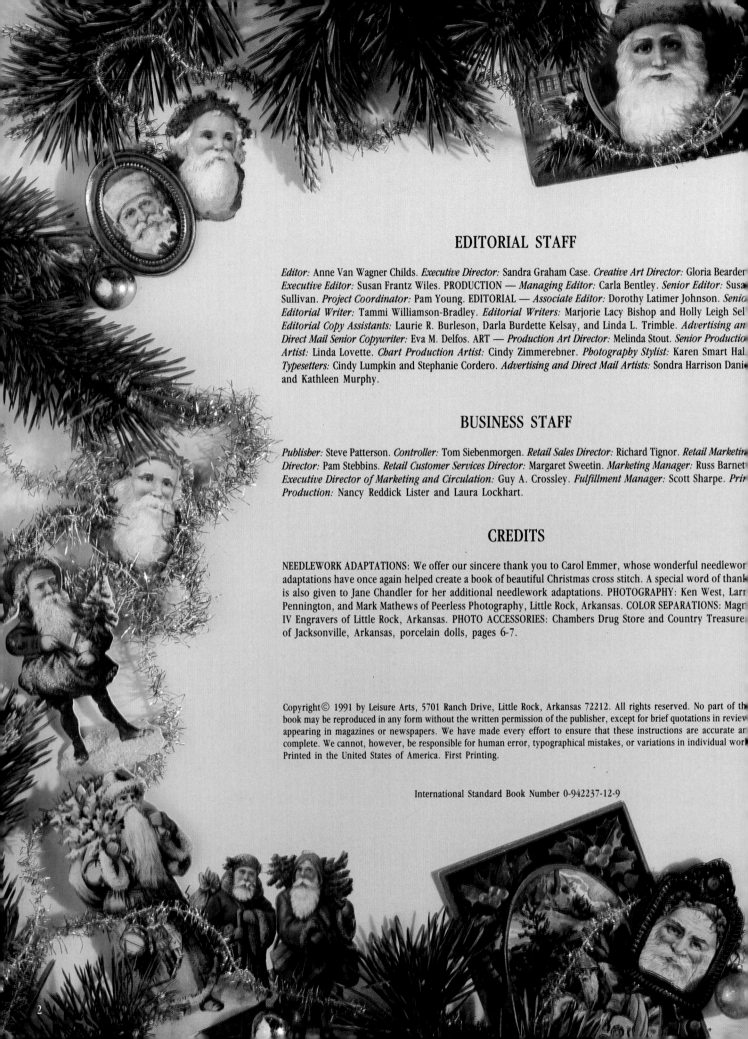

TABLE OF CONTENTS

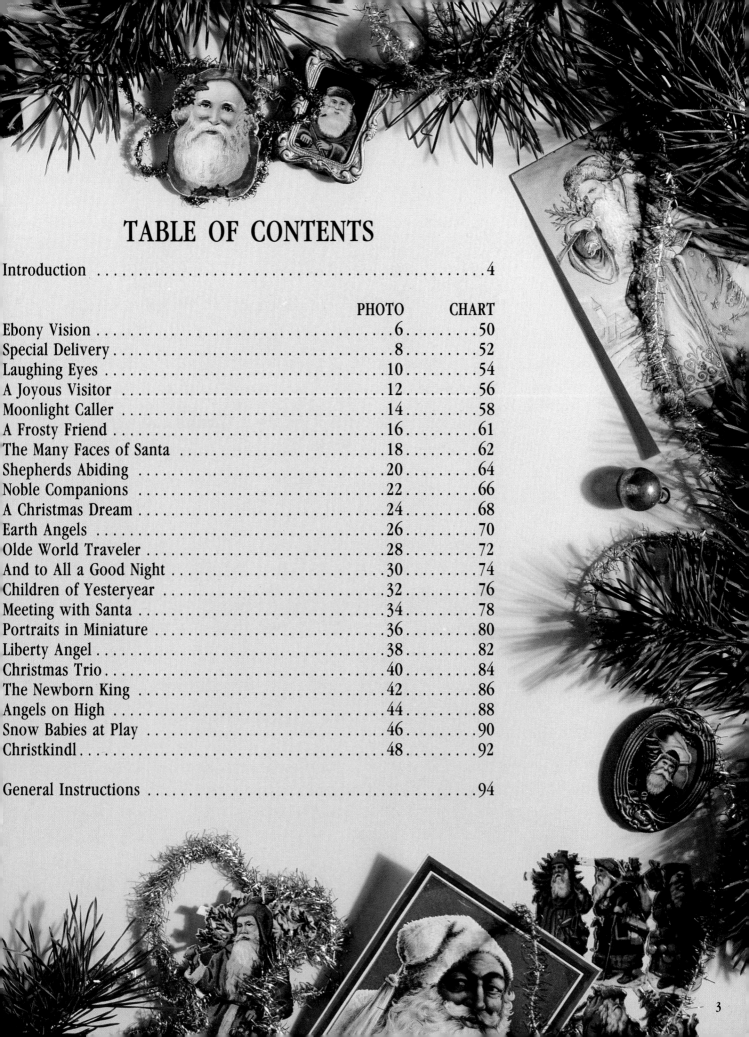

INTRODUCTION

Captured with care, portraits are windows in time, reflecting the spirit of their subjects and conveying a sense of warmth and vitality. Through them, our fondest memories are stirred, especially during the sentimental holiday season.

The Victorians left us a rich legacy of holiday portraiture in their beautiful Christmas cards and ornamental scraps. Perhaps it was their love of Christmas and the Yuletide characters that prompted them to commit their favorite likenesses to canvas. Among them we find the Holy Infant and the host of angels who heralded His birth, wide-eyed children hanging up their stockings, a wealth of jovial Santas, stately reindeer, and an assortment of little helpers ever ready to come to Santa's aid. Though these beautiful scenes are from another era, they have proven themselves to be timeless works of art.

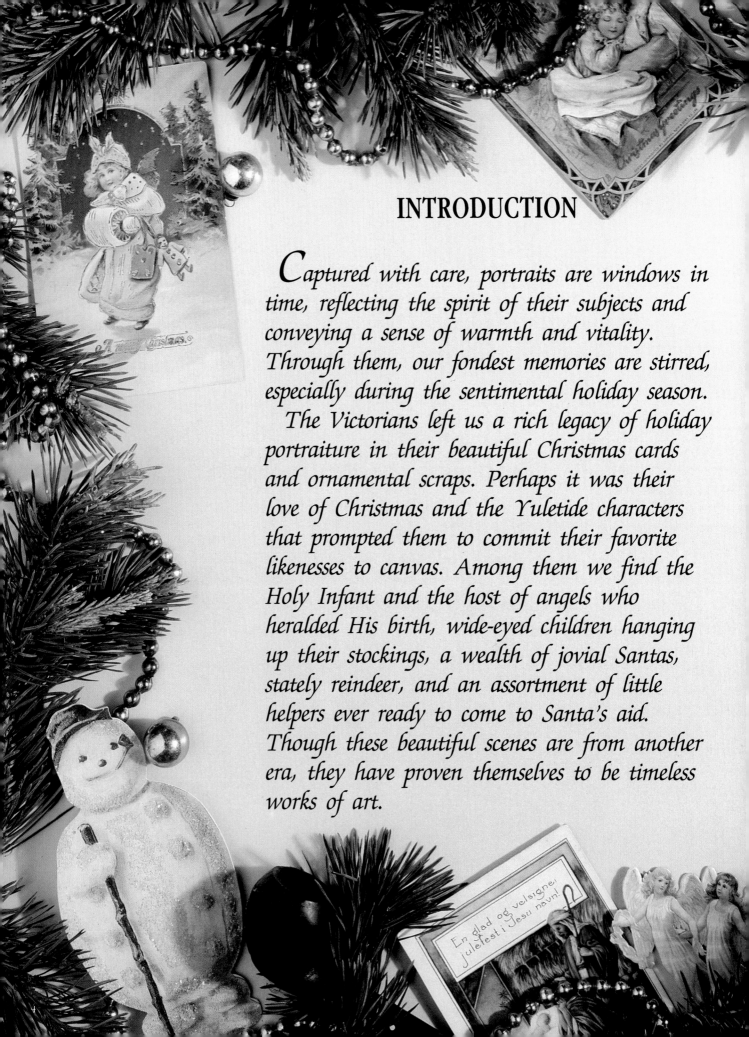

We still love these same wonderful characters today, and year after year, we take delight in bringing out their portraits at Christmastime to decorate our homes. The enduring symbols have become like old friends who provide a precious bond with other generations who shared our love for the season.

In this book, we have adapted many of these beloved holiday characters to cross stitch from our collection of antique postcards and scraps. It is our wish that the designs will fill your home with Christmas cheer and make memorable gifts for your family and friends. May you experience the merriment of the season as you create your own delightful company of Christmas companions!

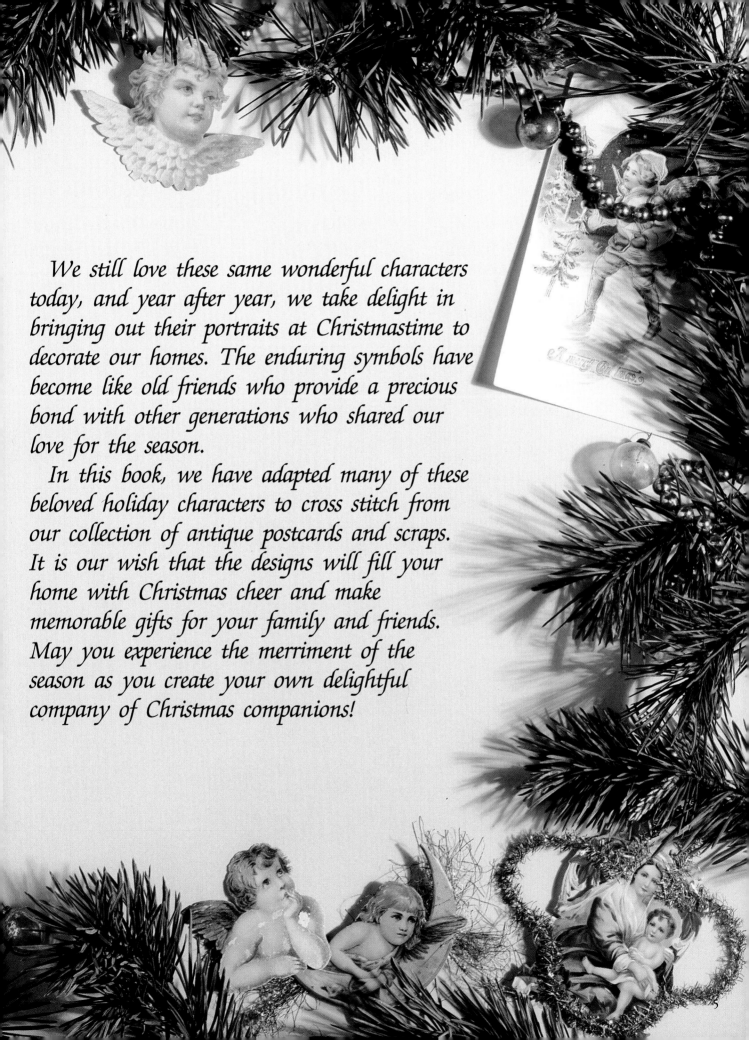

EBONY VISION

All of us hold in our hearts a unique image of Santa Claus as we believe him to be. But regardless of how we've portrayed him through the years, we've always endowed him with the wonderful qualities of benevolence and generosity. This rare ebony vision beautifully expresses Santa's universal spirit and appeal.

Chart on page 50

Chart on page 52

Special Delivery

Bearing gifts and news from near and far, the turn-of-the-century postman was as much a messenger of Christmas as today's Santa Claus. Children eagerly anticipated his arrival, squealing with delight as the postman produced letters and parcels from Grandma, Aunt Sally, and Momma's mail-order wish book. This roomy bag honoring the faithful mail carrier is wonderful for holding gifts until it's time to deliver them.

Laughing Eyes

Making children's wishes come true is Santa's greatest joy. Perhaps that's why we can spy a hint of merriment in his eyes when he arrives with his bag of toys. Magically, he always knows the right gift for every girl and boy — a shiny red wagon, a pretty doll, or a cuddly teddy to share their deepest secrets.

Chart on page 54

a joyous visitor

For centuries, artists have reverently created works reflecting adoration for the Christ Child. But it is not often in contemporary times that we see Him pictured with Christmas gift-givers such as Santa Claus or Old St. Nick. Such portrayals were common, however, at the turn of the century when this portrait was created. The joyous visitor kneeling beside the cradle here calls to mind St. Nicholas, the fourth century bishop who was legendary for his kindness and generosity.

Chart on page 56

Moonlight Caller

While the rest of the world sleeps, Santa makes his annual rounds, pausing in the moonlight atop each house to choose just the right toys for the children's stockings below. It is said that the custom of hanging Christmas stockings by the chimney stems from the time St. Nicholas helped a poor father who couldn't provide marriage dowries for his three daughters. As the legend goes, the good saint, in an effort to remain anonymous, went to their home in the middle of the night and tossed three bags of gold down the chimney. Miraculously, a bag landed in each of the girls' stockings, which had been hung from the mantel to dry. Since that time, children the world over have pinned up their stockings and awaited his late-night visit with hopefulness and excitement.

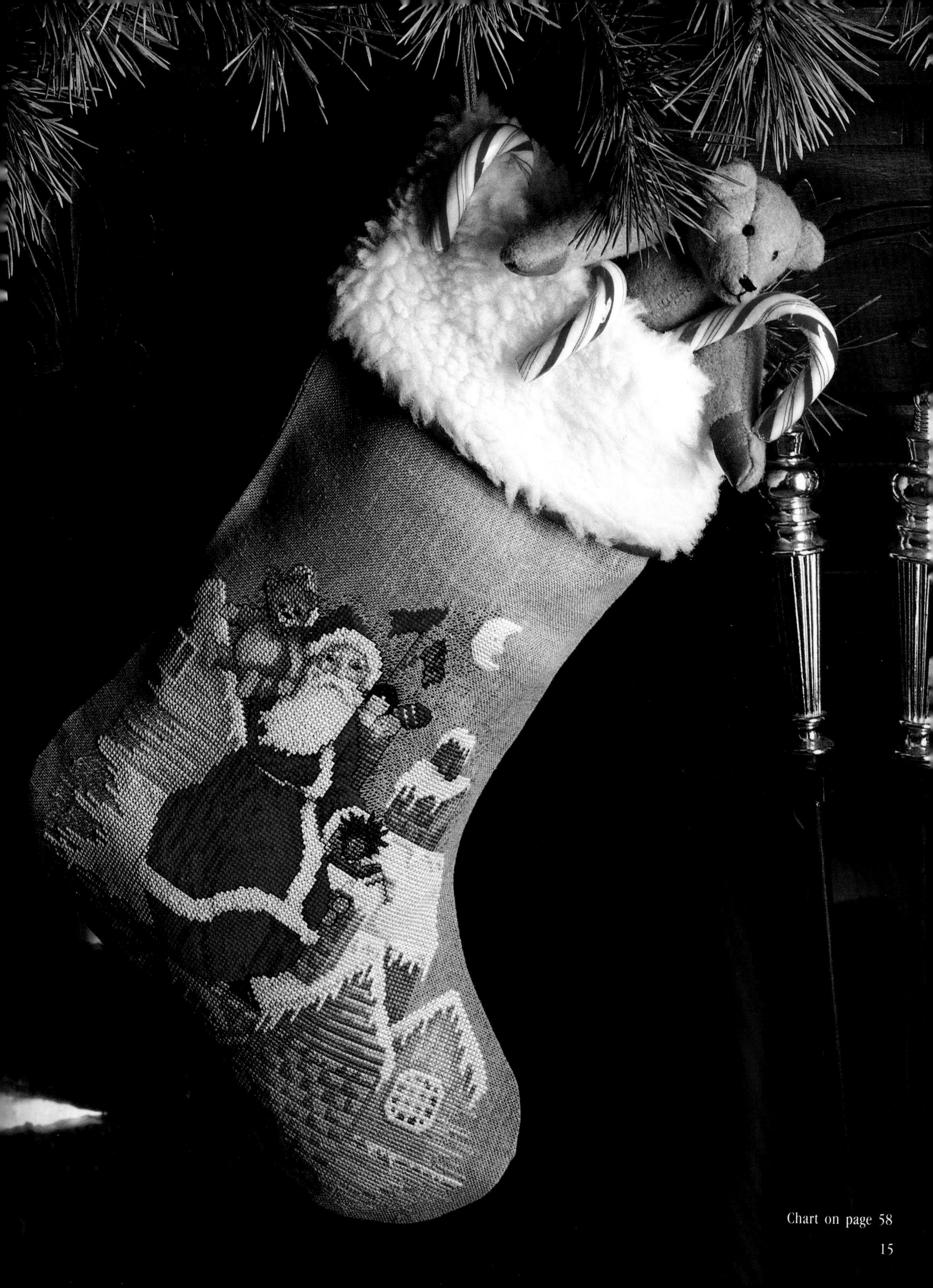

Chart on page 58

a frosty friend

As winter's first snowflakes drift to the ground, memories are stirred of those childhood days spent sculpting the perfect snowman. One can almost hear the laughter of children as their mitten-clad hands roll and pat the soft snow into the roly-poly shape of a frosty friend. Adding twig arms and coal-black eyes, they bring him to life and offer him warmth with a woolen scarf and hat. And although their jolly companion will soon disappear under the sun's bright rays, it's comforting to know that as long as there are young imaginations and snow, there will always be snowmen.

Chart on page 61

the many faces of santa

A snow-frosted traveler ... a richly robed bishop ... a holly-crowned merrymaker — these are only a few of the many faces of Santa Claus. And yet despite his myriad images, throughout history this ambassador of love has been an important constant to people everywhere. Always bearing gifts and good wishes, he represents the joy and warmth of Christmas. As we use these caring faces to adorn ornaments and gifts that anyone would love to find under the tree, we surround those we love with that wonderful holiday feeling.

Charts on page 6

Shepherds Abiding

And there were in the same country shepherds abiding in the field, keeping watch over their flock by night. And, lo, the angel of the Lord came upon them, and the glory of the Lord shone round about them: and they were sore afraid. And the angel said unto them, Fear not: for, behold, I bring you good tidings of great joy, which shall be to all people. For unto you is born this day in the city of David a Saviour, which is Christ the Lord. And this shall be a sign unto you; Ye shall find the babe wrapped in swaddling clothes, lying in a manger.

— LUKE 2:8-12

Ye shall find the babe
wrapped in swaddling clothes,
lying in a
manger.
LUKE 2:12

Chart on page

n page 66

NOBLE COMPANIONS

Of all the beasts that begged to do him service, Claus liked the reindeer best. "You shall go with me in my travels, for henceforth I shall bear my treasures not only to the children of the North, but to the children in every land whither the star points me and where the cross is lifted up!" So said Claus to the reindeer, and the reindeer neighed joyously and stamped their hoofs impatiently, as though they longed to start immediately.

— EUGENE FIELD

A Christmas Dream

On the night before Christmas, children fall asleep dreaming of Santa, secure in the belief that when they awaken he will have filled their stockings with wondrous treasures. And what sweeter visions are there to lull them to sleep than his bundle of toys and yummy sugarplums!

Chart on page 68

Earth Angels

Be not forgetful to entertain strangers: for thereby some have entertained angels unawares.

— *HEBREWS 13:2*

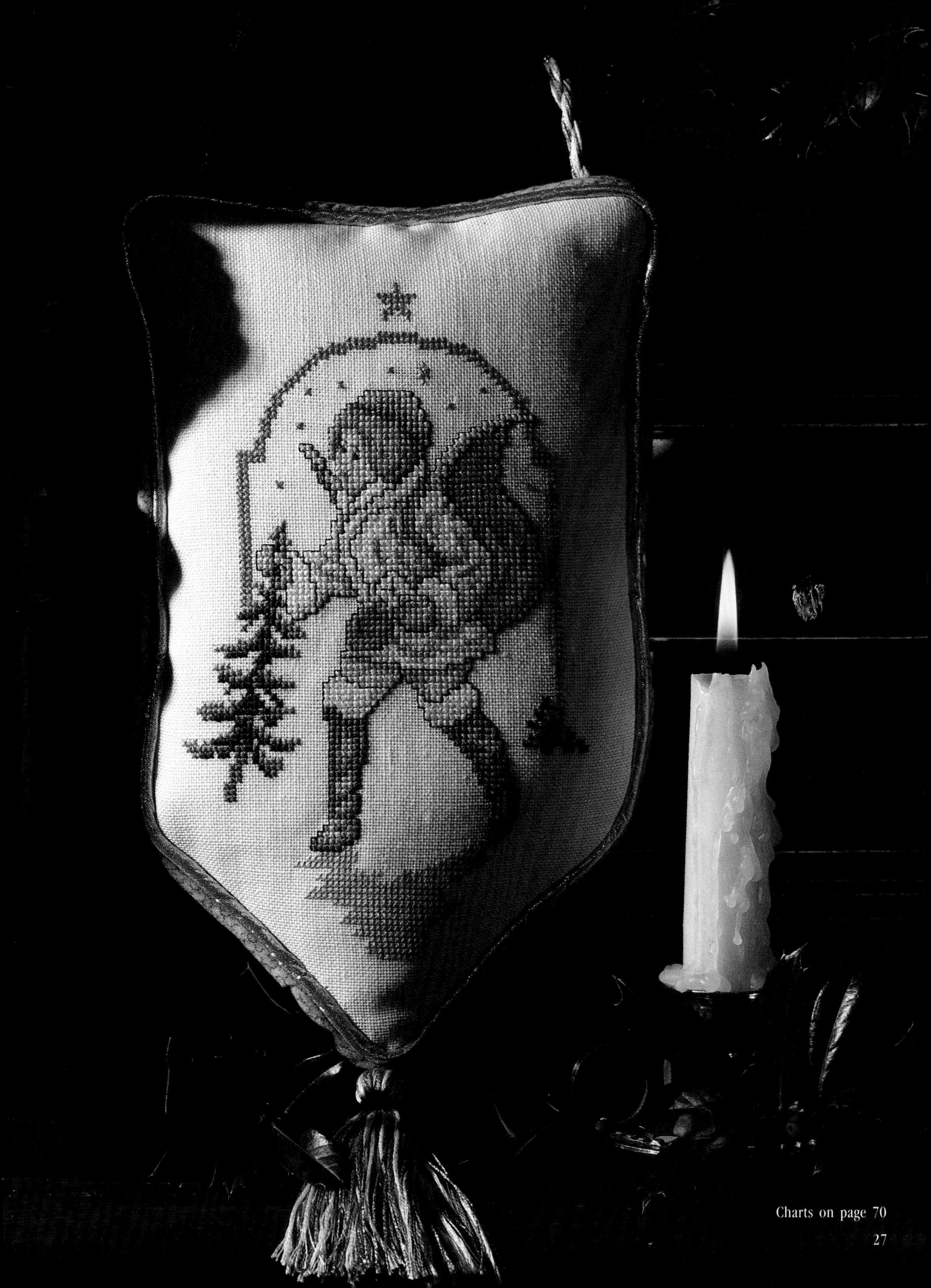

Charts on page 70

Olde World Traveler

He comes — the brave old Christmas!
His sturdy steps I hear;
We will give him a hearty welcome,
For he comes but once a year!

— MARY HOWITT

Chart o

and to all a good night

Flying through the starlit sky in a reindeer-drawn sleigh, this holiday traveler encompasses all the enchantment of our traditional American Santa Claus. From his airborne mode of travel and familiar red suit to his marvelously merry nature, today's gift-giver is a unique blending of the traditions and beliefs of the immigrants who settled this land.

Chart on page 74

Children of Yesteryear

Ever since the Victorians made elaborately decorated trees a part of their Christmas celebration, children have delighted in helping to trim the branches with beautiful ornaments and shimmering lights. Sharing in this beloved tradition is just one of the wonderful ways our lives are enriched each holiday season. Such moments of joy, preserved in a collection of photographs, become a cherished Christmas chronicle!

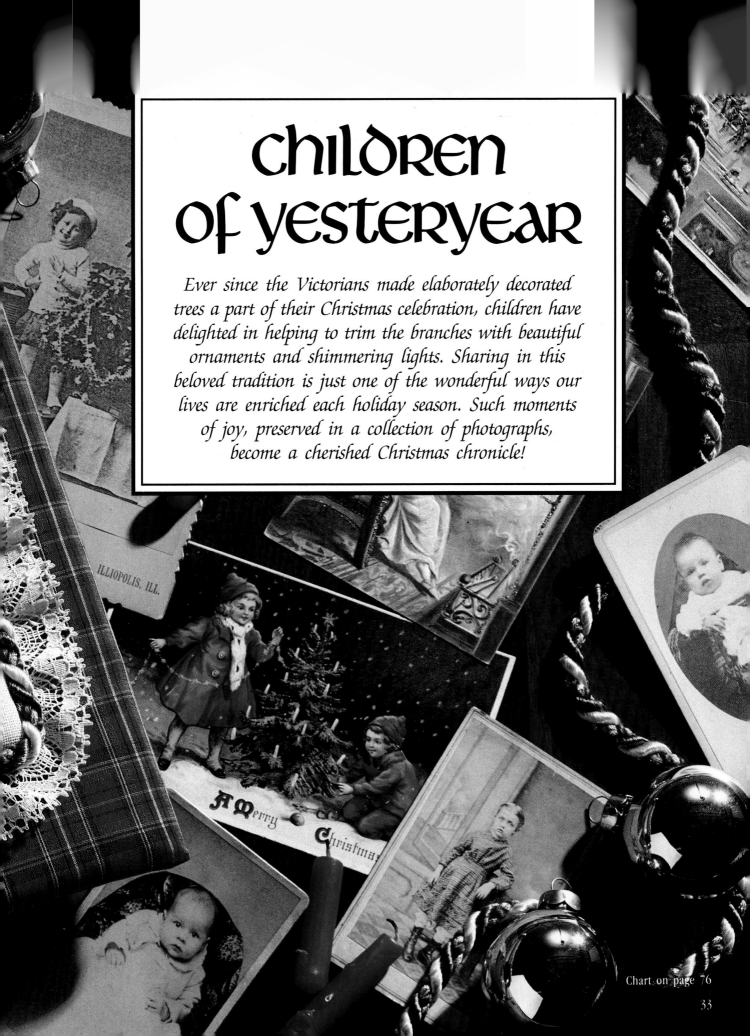

Chart on page 76

meeting with santa

The thrill of visiting with Santa brings delight to children of all ages. A spirit of gaiety and good cheer fills the air as the youngsters vie for the chance to touch the kindly old gentleman and whisper in his ear. And as he takes a moment to hear each child's Christmas wish, Santa's jubilant laughter and broad smile convey his excitement at meeting with them, too.

Chart on page 78

Portraits in Miniature

Holiday ornaments are often the tiniest of Christmas keepsakes. As each diminutive trinket is unpacked and nestled lovingly among the branches of an evergreen tree, memories of joyful seasons past rush to embrace us again. For your enjoyment, we've assembled this enchanting collection of miniature pillow ornaments adorned with some of the most beloved players in the Yuletide drama.

Charts on page 80

LIBERTY ANGEL

Christmas is a time for us to count our blessings and reflect on the things we hold dear — family, friends, God, and country. By blending images of patriotism with traditional symbols of the holiday season, we are inspired to believe that peace on earth is a Christmas message for today, tomorrow, and always.

Chart on page 82

CHRISTMAS TRIO

Because Santa can't be everywhere at once, he often enlists the aid of special friends to help him in his merry mission. Tiny elves and gnomes have been known to lend their tree-trimming skills, leaving behind touches of gold as a sign of their handiwork. Benevolent angels visiting from above delight in spreading Christmas cheer. Whether delivered by Santa or one of these faithful helpers, the treasures tucked inside your stocking are sure to be just what you've been wishing for.

Charts on page 84

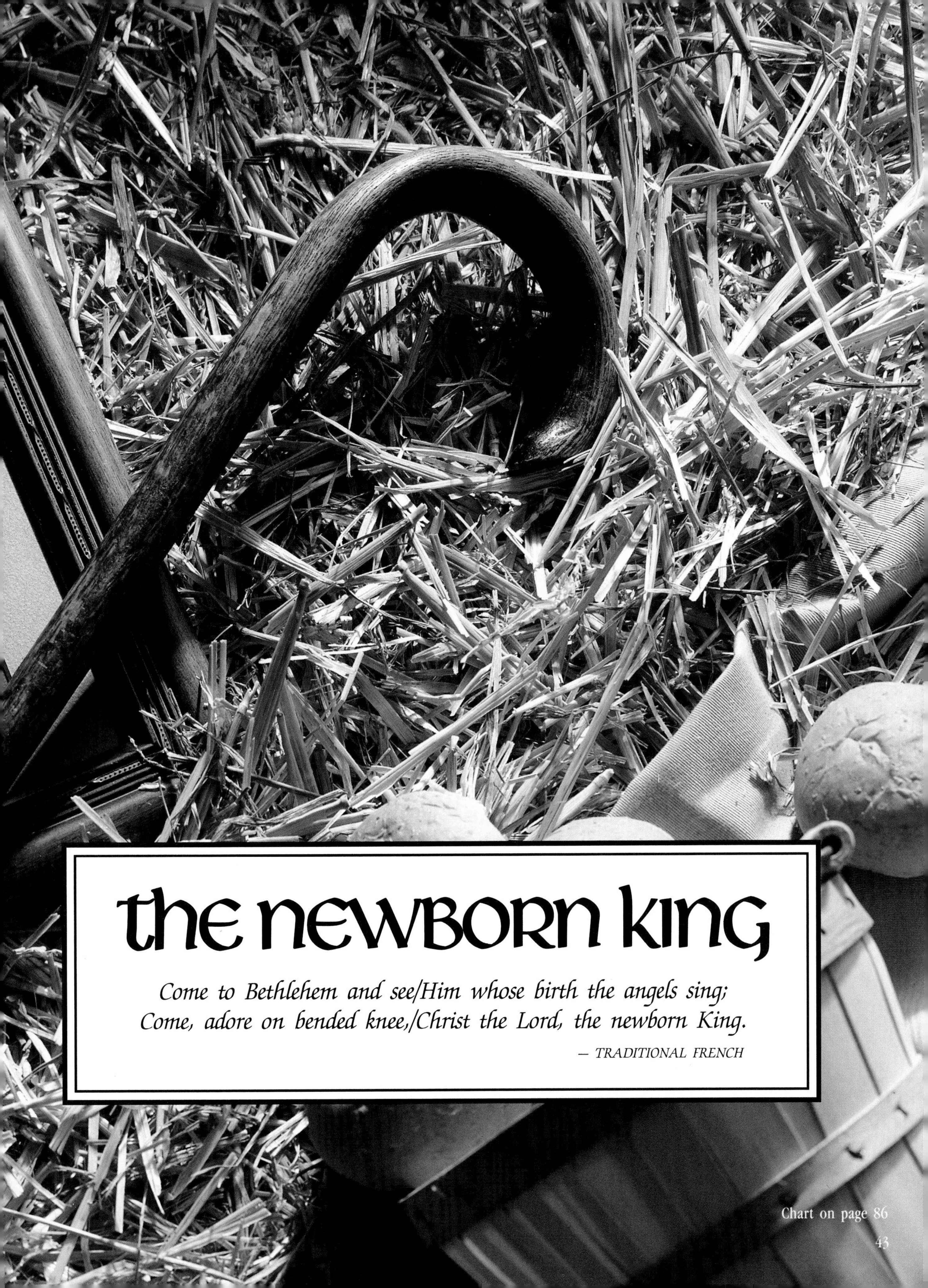

The Newborn King

Come to Bethlehem and see/Him whose birth the angels sing;
Come, adore on bended knee,/Christ the Lord, the newborn King.

— TRADITIONAL FRENCH

Chart on page 86

angels on high

Angels we have heard on high,/Sweetly singing o'er the plains,
And the mountains in reply,/Echoing their joyous strains
Gloria in excelsis Deo.

TRADITIONAL FRENCH

Chart on page 88

Snow Babies at Play

Sledding and tumbling about on wintry slopes, snow babies are as popular today as they were in the early 1900's. The chubby toddlers lighten our hearts with their playful antics and lead us to recall our own youthful days of frosty fun. Bundled from head to toe, the endearing characters also remind us that snowy winter days are the perfect time for snuggling under a warm wrap.

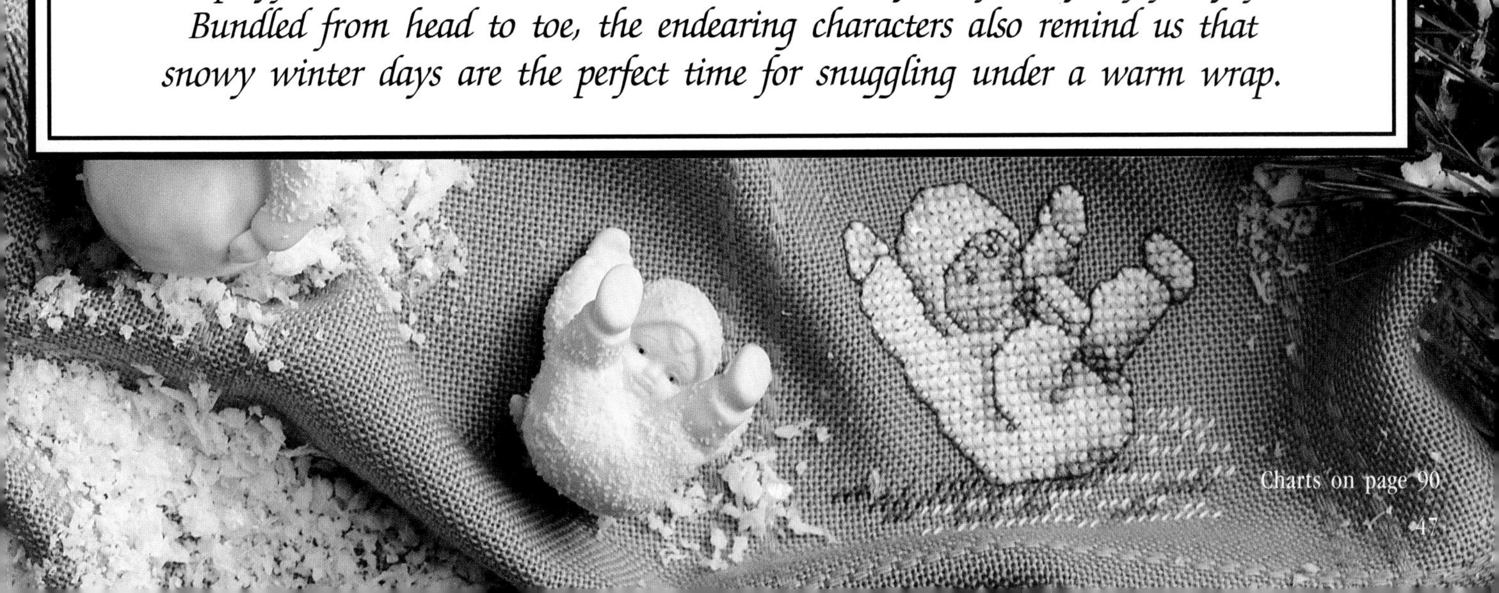

Charts on page 90

Christkindl

During the joyous Christmas season, we celebrate the birth of Jesus and His gift of everlasting life. In some European countries, His benevolence is personified by the golden-haired Christkindl (meaning Christ Child), an angelic gift-bearer who is believed to be sent from heaven at Christmastime. Finished as a moon and a star, these touching designs symbolize the Child's heavenly connection.

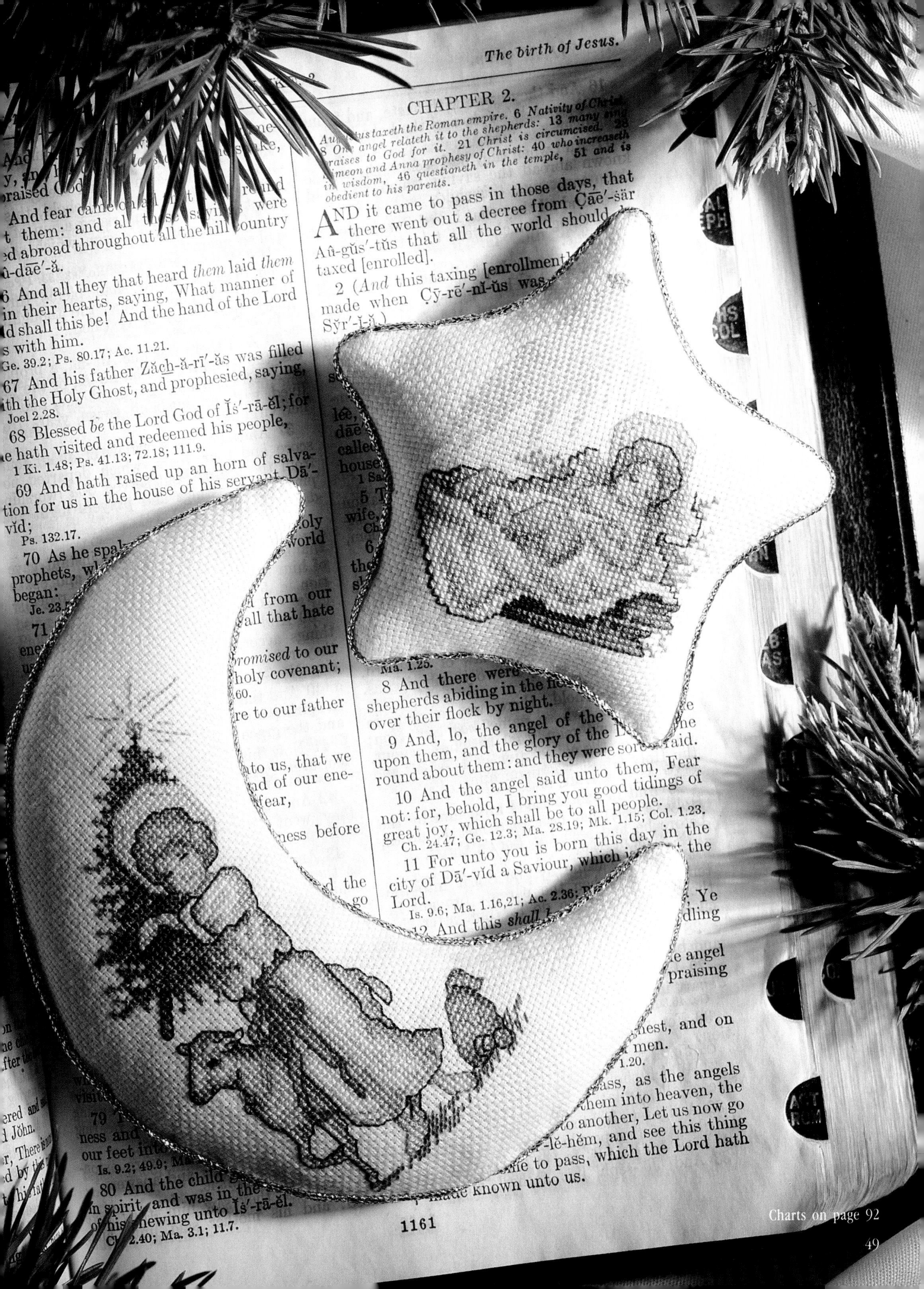

Charts on page 92

Ebony Vision

DMC	X	¼X	B'ST
gold metallic & 729*	✓		
blanc	✓	✓	✓
309	✓		
326	✓		
335	✓		
355	✓		
356	✓	✓	✓
469	✓		
470	✓		
471	✓		
524	✓	✓	
632	✓	✓	✓
640	✓	✓	
642	✓	✓	
644	✓	✓	
645	✓		
646	✓		
676	✓		
677	✓		
680	✓	✓	
712			
729	✓		
754	✓	✓	
758	✓	✓	
760	✓	✓	
815			✓
822	✓	✓	
838	✓	✓	
839	✓	✓	
844	✓	✓	
899	✓		
930	✓	✓	
931	✓	✓	
936	✓		
937	✓		
938	✓	✓	✓
948	✓	✓	
950	✓	✓	
951	✓	✓	
3371	✓	✓	✓
3772	✓	✓	
3773	✓	✓	
3779	✓	✓	
3328			✓

Blue area indicates last row of top section of design.

* Use one strand gold metallic and two strands 729.

STITCH COUNT (87w x 131h)

Aida 11	8"	x	12"
Lugana 25 over 2	7"	x	10½"
Aida 14	6¼"	x	9⅜"
Aida 18	4⅞"	x	7⅜"
Hardanger 22	4"	x	6"

Ebony Vision (shown on page 7) was stitched over 2 fabric threads on a 15" x 19" piece of Mushroom Lugana (25 ct). Three strands of floss were used for Cross Stitch and 1 strand for Backstitch. It was custom framed.

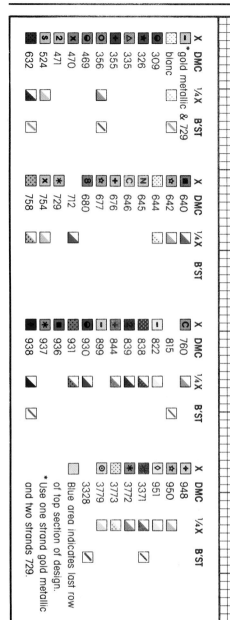

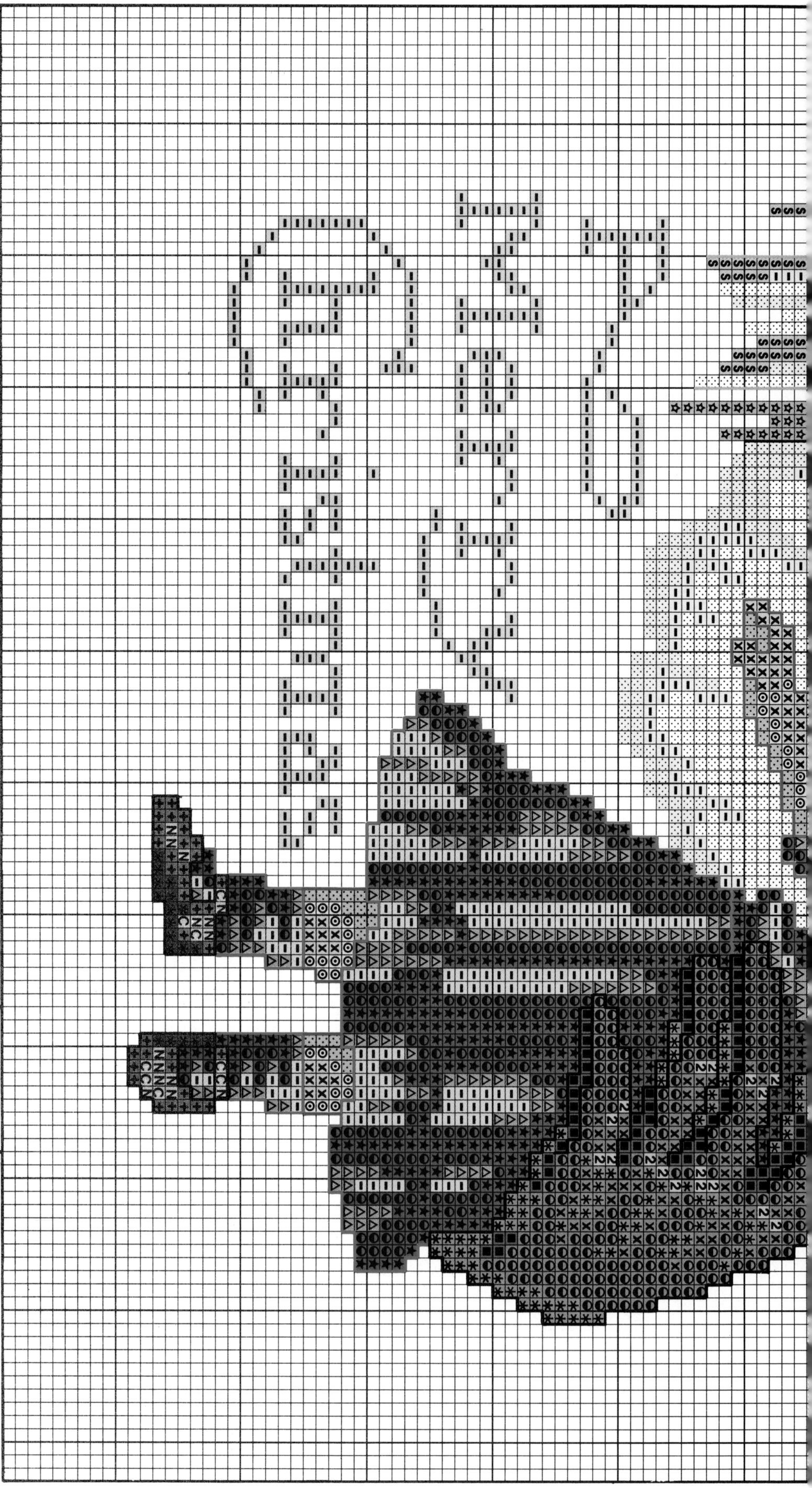

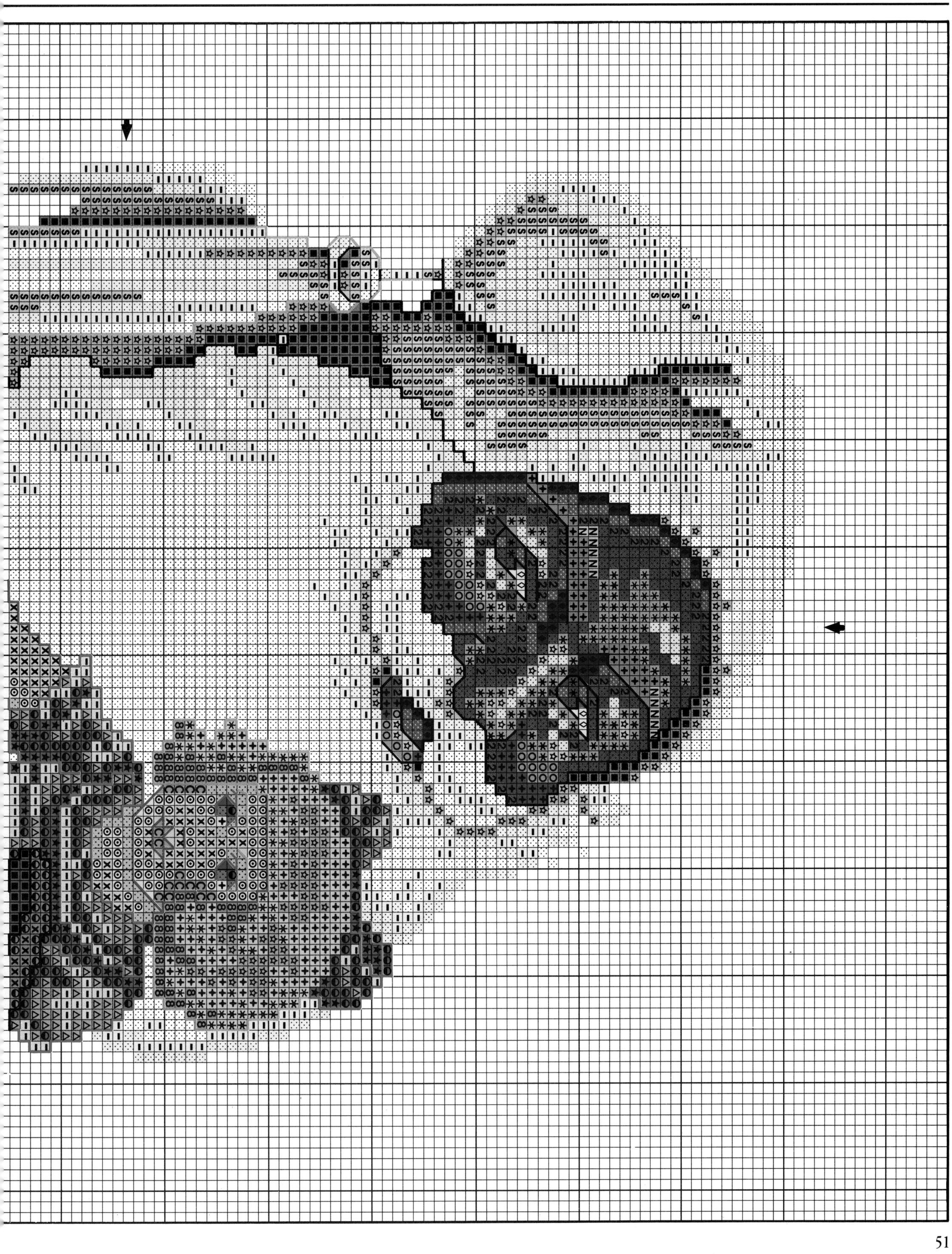

special delivery

Special Delivery (shown on page 8) was stitched over 2 fabric threads on a 15" x 19" piece of Driftwood Dublin Linen (25 ct). Three strands of floss were used for Cross Stitch, 2 strands for gold metallic Backstitch, and 1 strand for all other stitches. It was made into a gift bag.

For gift bag, trim stitched piece 2" larger than design on all sides.

For cording, cut one 2½" x 53" bias strip of coordinating fabric. Lay purchased cord along center of strip on wrong side of fabric; matching raw edges, fold strip over cord. Using zipper foot, baste along length of strip close to cord; trim seam allowance to ½". Matching raw edges and beginning at bottom center of stitched piece, pin cording to right side of stitched piece. Ends of cording should overlap approximately 2"; pin overlapping end out of the way.

Starting 2" from beginning end of cording and ending 4" from overlapping end, sew cording to stitched piece. On overlapping end of cording, remove 2½" of basting; fold end of fabric back and trim cord so that it meets beginning end of cord. Fold end of fabric under ½"; wrap fabric over beginning end of cording. Finish sewing cording to stitched piece. Clip seam allowance at corners. Turn seam allowance to wrong side of stitched piece and press.

For bag bottom, cut one 18" square of fabric. Fold fabric in half from top to bottom and again from left to right. To mark cutting line, tie one end of an 11" length of string to a fabric marking pencil. Insert a thumbtack through the string 8" from pencil. Insert thumbtack in fabric as shown in **Fig. 1** and mark one-fourth of a circle. Follow pencil line and cut through all thicknesses.

Fig. 1

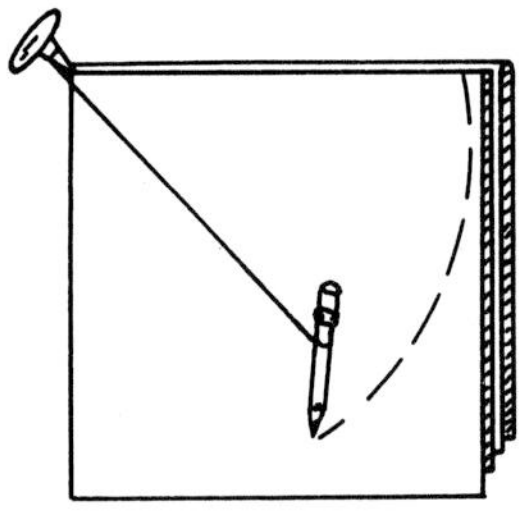

For bag sides, cut one 51" x 39" piece of fabric. Matching wrong side of stitched piece to right side of bag, center stitched piece on fabric with 4" between bottom of stitched piece and edge of one long side (**Fig. 2**); pin in place. Using zipper foot and same color thread as cording, attach stitched piece to bag by sewing as close as possible to cording, taking care not to catch fabric of stitched piece.

STITCH COUNT (96w x 146h)

Aida 11	8¾"	x	13⅜"
Linen 25 over 2	7¾"	x	11¾"
Aida 14	6⅞"	x	10½"
Aida 18	5⅜"	x	8⅛"
Hardanger 22	4⅜"	x	6¾"

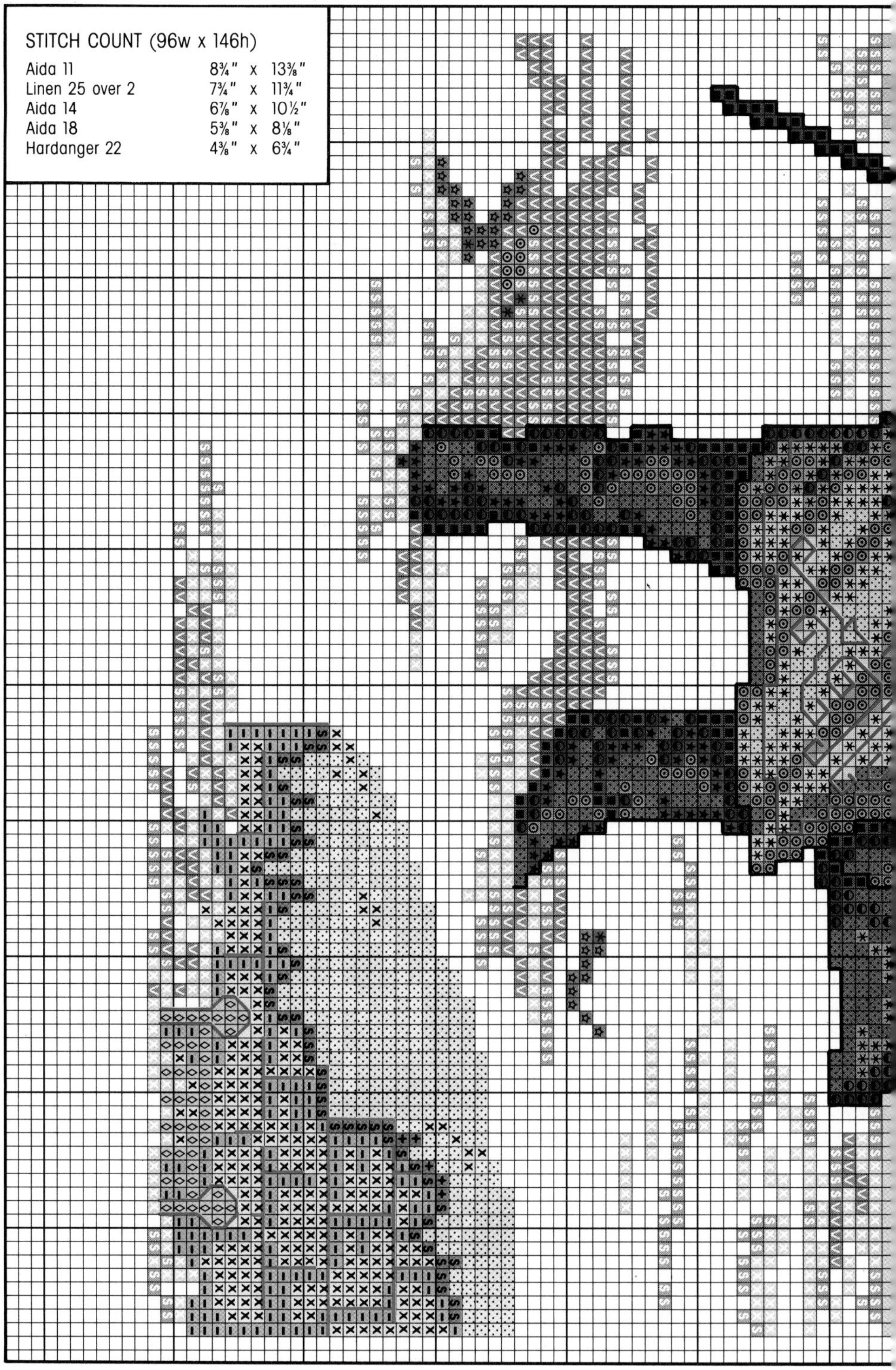

Fig. 2

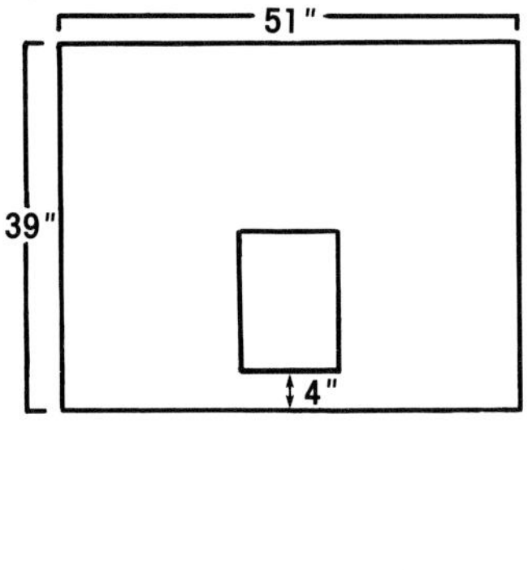

Matching right sides and short edges, fold fabric in half. Use a ½" seam allowance to sew fabric piece together along side opposite fold.

Matching right sides and raw edges, pin bag bottom to bottom of bag sides; clip seam allowance of bag bottom if needed for proper fit. Use a ½" seam allowance to sew fabric pieces together.

Turn raw edge of bag to wrong side ½"; turn under ½" again and hem. Turn bag right side out. Tie leather strap around top of bag.

X	DMC	¼X	½X	B'ST
⁘	blanc	✓	✓	
✱	321			
■	433	✓		
◒	434	✓		
C	435			
◎	470			
V	610			
★	611			
☆	612			
◇	613			
S	640	✓	✓	✓
–	642	✓		✓
X	644	✓		
N	754	✓		
4	758	✓		
⁘	822	✓	✓	✓
▩	838	✓		
▫	839	✓		
◒	924	✓		
O	926	✓	✓	
★	936	✓		
☆	937			
X	962			
◒	3021	✓		
◎	3022		V	
✱	3023		S	
⁘	3024			
◆	3064	✓		
■	3371	✓		✓
✱	3768	✓	✓	
⁘	3779	✓		
▩	3787	✓		
+	3790			
◇	gold metallic	✓		✓

Pink area indicates last row of top section of design.

laughing eyes

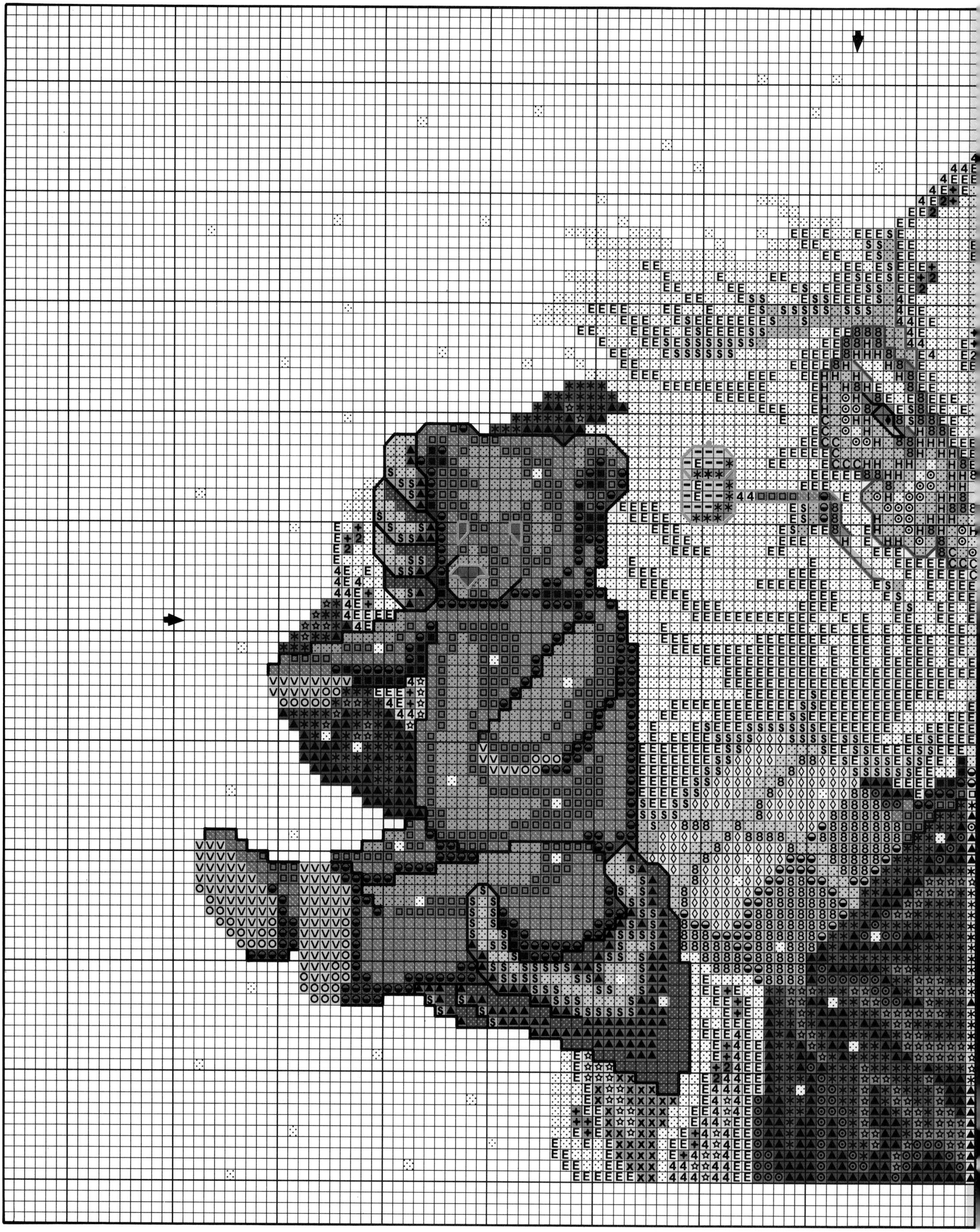

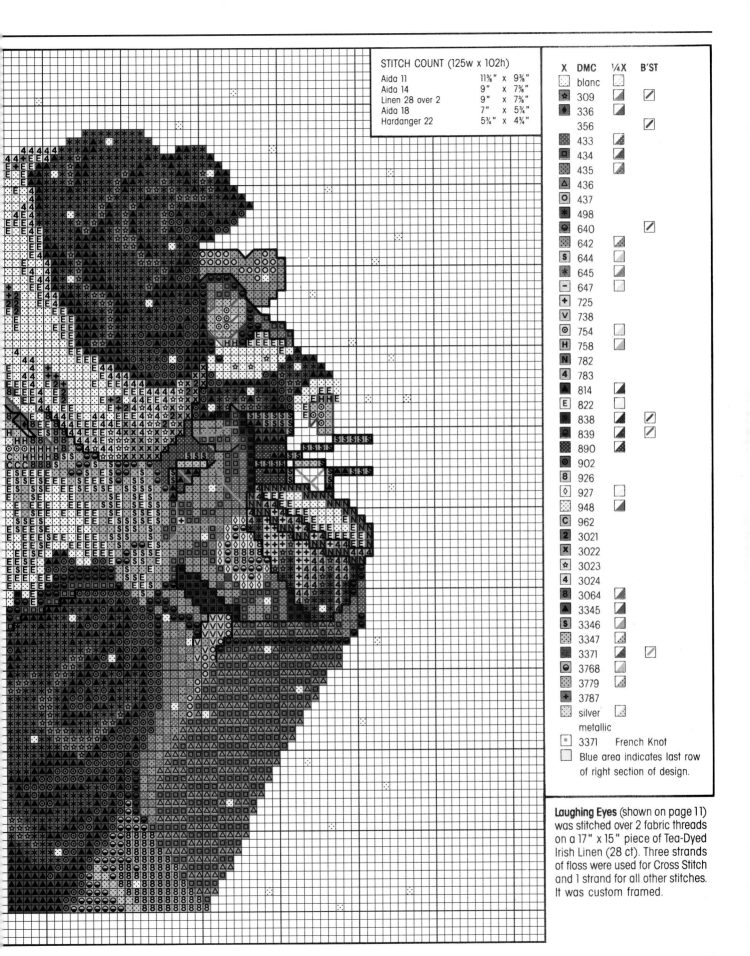

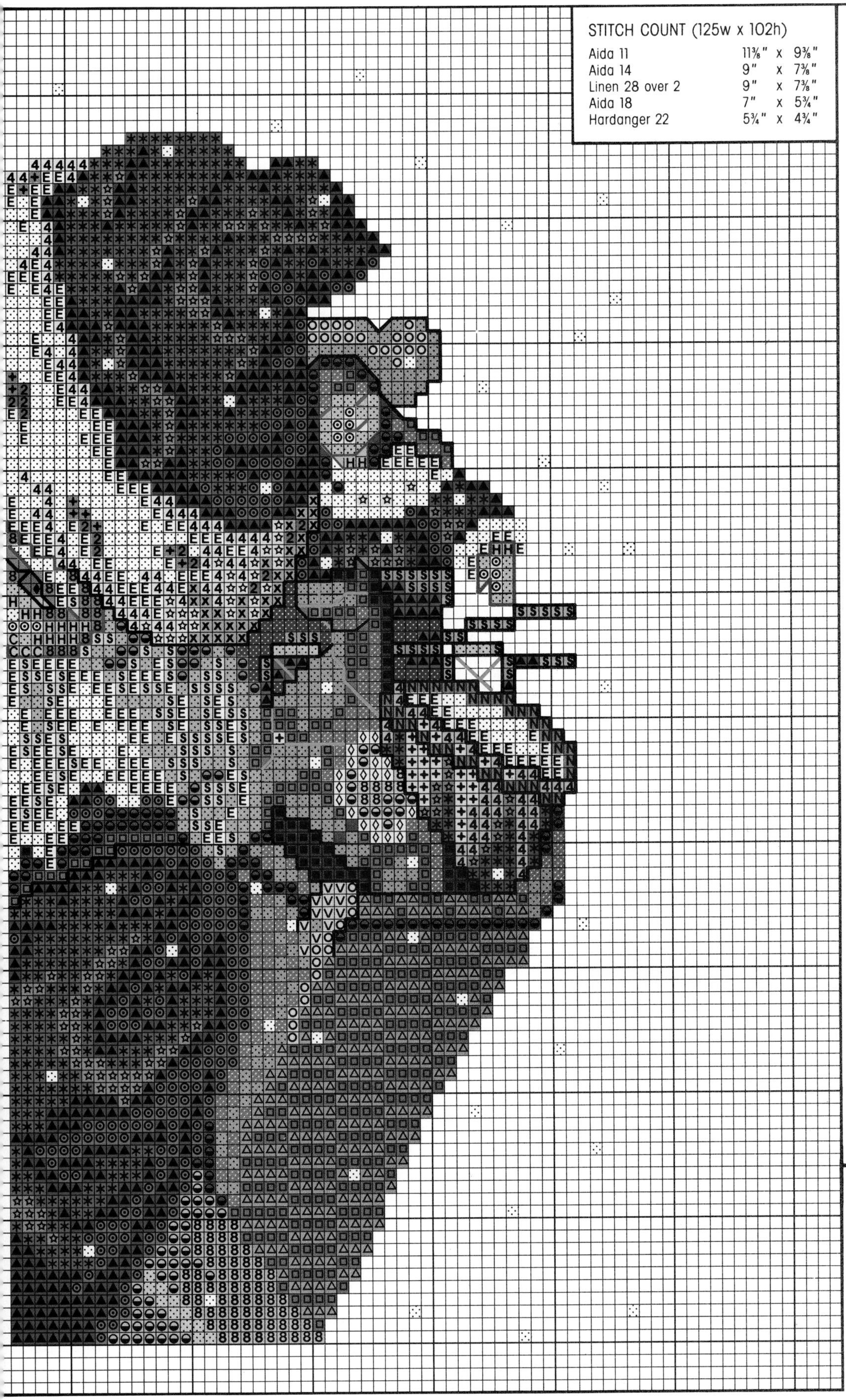

STITCH COUNT (125w x 102h)			
Aida 11	11⅜"	x	9⅜"
Aida 14	9"	x	7⅜"
Linen 28 over 2	9"	x	7⅜"
Aida 18	7"	x	5¾"
Hardanger 22	5¾"	x	4¾"

X	DMC	¼X	B'ST
	blanc	■	
	309	■	/
	336	■	
	356		/
	433	■	
	434	■	
	435	■	
	436		
	437		
	498		
	640		/
	642	■	
S	644	■	
	645	■	
-	647	■	
+	725		
V	738		
	754	■	
H	758	■	
N	782		
4	783		
	814	■	
E	822	■	
	838	■	/
	839	■	/
	890	■	
	902		
8	926		
	927	■	
	948	■	
C	962		
2	3021		
X	3022		
	3023		
4	3024		
8	3064	■	
	3345	■	
S	3346	■	
	3347	■	
	3371	■	/
	3768	■	
	3779	■	
	3787		
	silver metallic	■	
•	3371 French Knot		
	Blue area indicates last row of right section of design.		

Laughing Eyes (shown on page 11) was stitched over 2 fabric threads on a 17" x 15" piece of Tea-Dyed Irish Linen (28 ct). Three strands of floss were used for Cross Stitch and 1 strand for all other stitches. It was custom framed.

a joyous visitor

X	DMC	¼X	½X	B'ST
	blanc	■		
	319	■		
□	320	■		
◇	353			
☆	367	■		■
◎	368	■		
▶	433	■		
3	434	■		■
	435	■		
4	436	■		
☆	437	■		
◆	610			
H	611			
△	612			
	632			■
◇	640	■		
×	642	■		
I	644	■		
☆	727	■		
	754	■		
◆	758	■		
●	801	■		■
	822	■		
▶	890	■		
◎	962			
■	3031		■	
	3064	■		
V	3078	■		
	3371			■
	3779	■		

Blue area indicates last row of top section of design.

STITCH COUNT (76w x 106h)			
Aida 11	7"	x	9¾"
Aida 14	5½"	x	7⅝"
Linen 32 over 2	4¾"	x	6⅝"
Aida 18	4¼"	x	6"
Hardanger 22	3½"	x	4⅞"

A Joyous Visitor (shown on page 13) was stitched over 2 fabric threads on a 13" x 15" piece of Raw Belfast Linen (32 ct). Two strands of floss were used for Cross Stitch and 1 strand for all other stitches. It was custom framed.

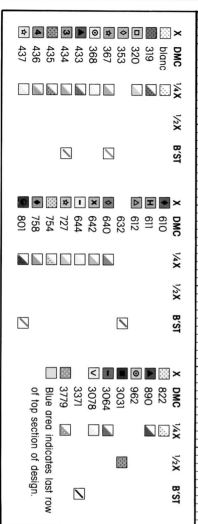

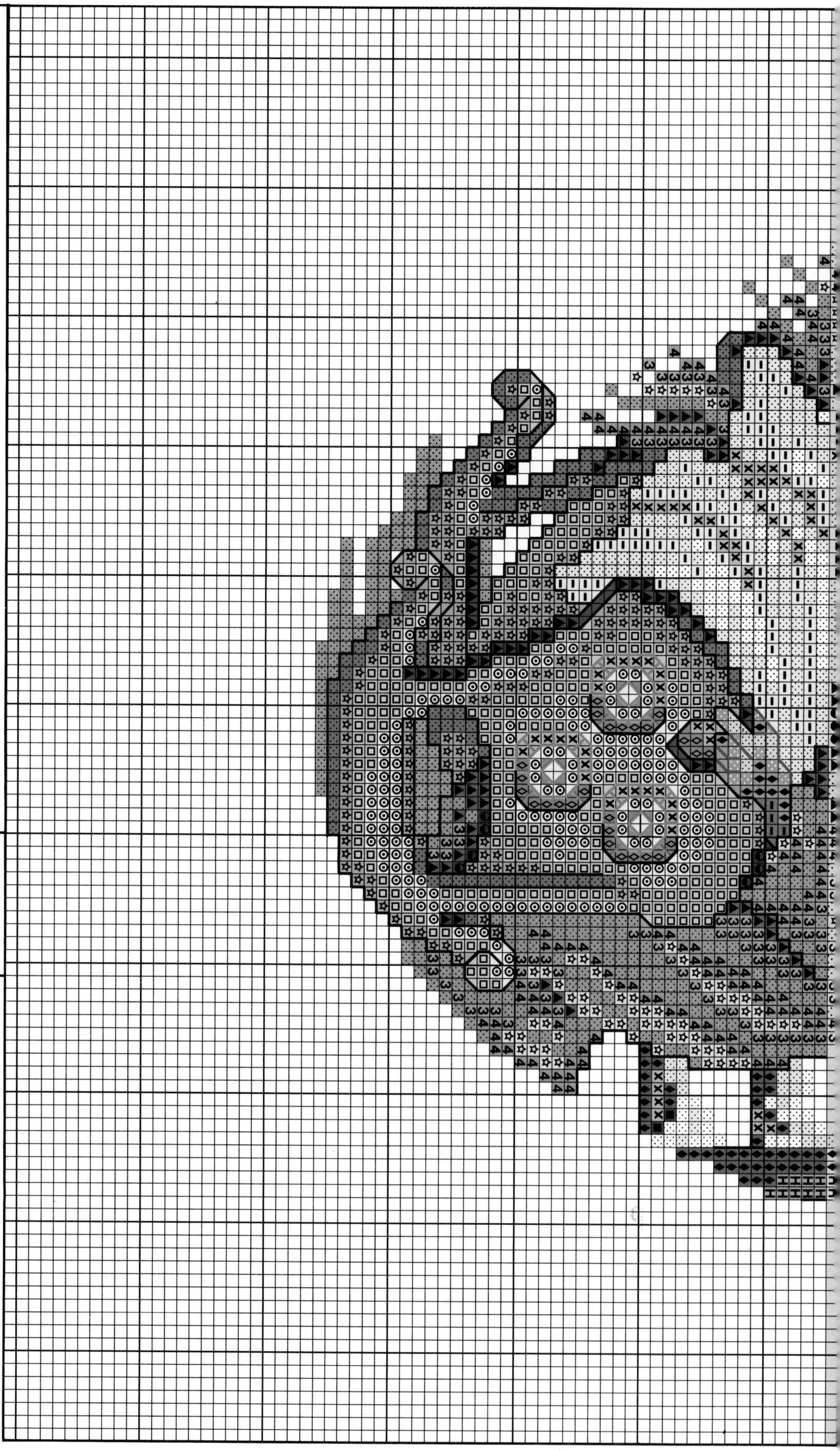

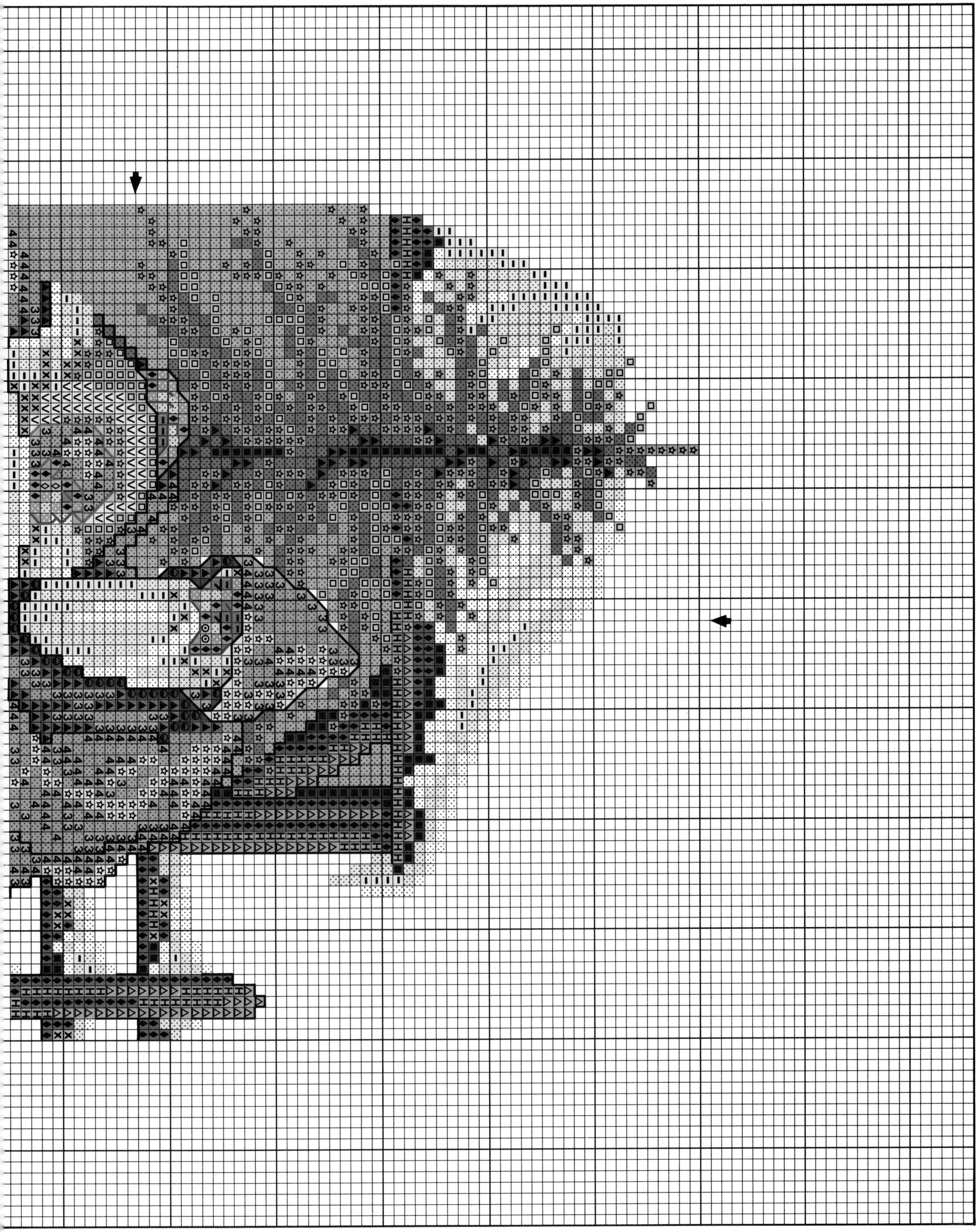

moonlight caller

X	DMC	¼X	½X	B'ST
	blanc	✓		
	311			
S	312	✓		
V	317	✓	✓	
	318			
	319			
	320			
x	322	✓		
	349			✓
	367			
	413	✓	✓	
-	415			
	420	✓	✓	
2	498			
	632	✓		
	640	✓		✓
	642	✓		
A	644	✓		
	754	✓		
x	758	✓		
s	760	✓		
	814	✓		
*	817			
C	822	✓	✓	✓
	869	✓		
	948	✓		
	950		✓	
H	962	✓		
	3045	✓	✓	
3	3046	✓		
	3047	✓		✓
	3064	✓		
	3371			✓
	3770	✓		✓
	3772			
	3773		✓	✓
	3799	✓		
	gold metallic	✓		✓

Blue area indicates last row of top section of design.

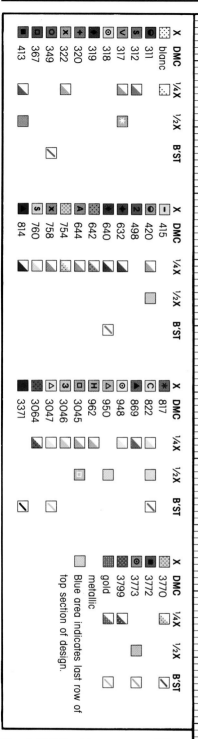

Moonlight Caller (shown on page 15) was stitched over 2 fabric threads on a 14" x 21" piece of Raw Belfast Linen (32 ct). Two strands of floss were used for Cross Stitch and 1 strand for all other stitches. It was made into a stocking (see Stocking instructions, page 60).

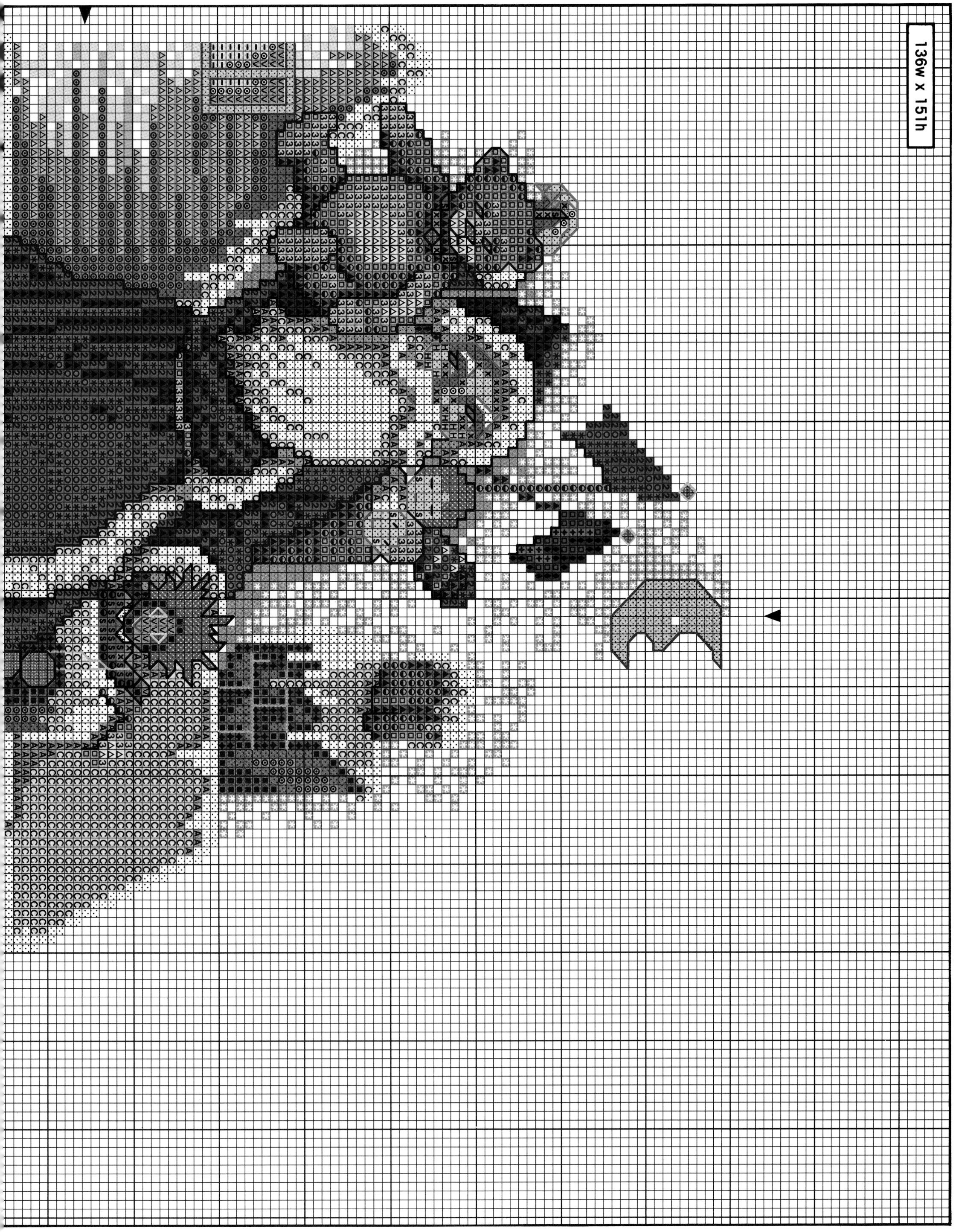
136w x 151h

Moonlight Caller
Chart on page 58.

For stocking, cut one 14" x 21" piece of Raw Belfast Linen for backing. For lining, cut two 14" x 21" pieces of brown fabric. For cuff front, cut one 5½" x 15" piece of off-white acrylic fur. For cuff backing, cut one 5½" x 15" piece of off-white fabric.

Matching arrows to form one pattern, trace entire stocking pattern onto tracing paper; cut out pattern. Matching right sides and raw edges, place stitched piece and backing fabric together. Place pattern on wrong side of stitched piece. Refer to photo to position pattern on design; pin pattern in place. Use fabric marking pencil to draw around pattern.

Leaving top edge open, sew stitched piece and backing fabric together directly on drawn line. Trim seam allowance to ½" and clip curves. Trim top edge along drawn line. Turn stocking right side out.

Repeat to draw around pattern and sew lining pieces together, sewing just inside drawn line. Trim seam allowance to ½" and clip curves. Trim top edge along drawn line. **Do not turn lining right side out.** Press top edge of lining ½" to wrong side.

Matching right sides and short edges, fold cuff front in half. Using a ½" seam allowance, sew along short edges. Repeat for cuff backing.

For cording, cut one 2" x 18" bias strip of red fabric. Center cording on wrong side of bias strip; matching long edges, fold strip over cord. Using zipper foot, baste along length of strip close to cord; trim sear allowance to ½". Matching raw edges and beginning at cuff seam, pi cording to right side of cuff front. Ends of cording should overla approximately 2"; pin overlapping end out of the way.

Starting 2" from beginning end of cording and ending 4" fron overlapping end, sew cording to cuff front.

On overlapping end of cording, remove 2½" of basting; fold end c fabric back and trim cord so that it meets beginning end of cord. Fol end of fabric under ½"; wrap fabric over beginning end of cording. Finis sewing cording to cuff front.

Matching right sides and raw edges, use a ½" seam allowance to se cuff front and cuff back together along edge with cording. Turn right sid out and press.

With right side of cuff front and wrong side of stocking facing, matc raw edges and use a ½" seam allowance to sew cuff to stocking. Fol cuff 3½" over stocking; press.

For hanger, cut one 1" x 6" strip of Belfast Linen. Press each long edg of strip ¼" to center. Matching long edges, fold strip in half and sew clos to folded edges. Matching short edges, fold hanger in half and whipstitc to inside of stocking at left seam.

With wrong sides facing, place lining inside stocking. Matching presse edge of lining to seam of cuff, whipstitch lining to stocking.

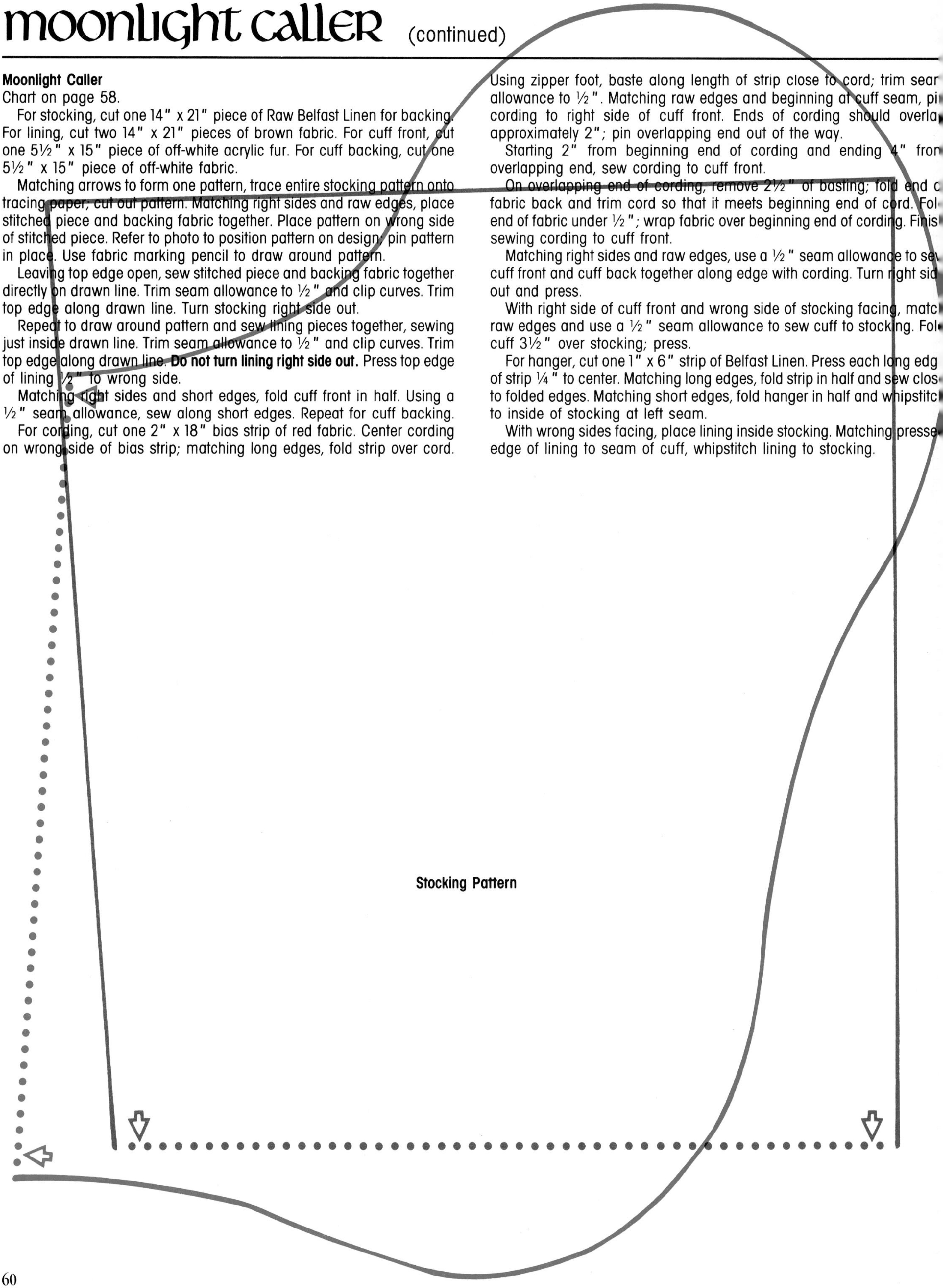

Stocking Pattern

A Frosty Friend

X	DMC	¼X	¾X	B'ST
⁘	blanc	✓	✓	
■	310	✓		✓
▫	434	✓		
⊙	436			
−	640			
♦	642	✓		
*	644	✓		
S	646			
2	822	✓		
+	844			✓

A Frosty Friend (shown on page 17) was stitched over an 8" x 12" piece of waste canvas (10 ct) on a 50" x 60" piece of plaid wool fabric. Five strands of floss were used for Cross Stitch and 2 strands for Backstitch. (See Working on Waste Canvas, page 94.) It was made into a stadium blanket.

For stadium blanket, machine stitch 3" away from all four edges of wool fabric. Fringe fabric to machine-stitched lines. Referring to Diagram, place the design diagonally in one corner with the bottom of the design 8" away from the corner of the stadium blanket.

DIAGRAM

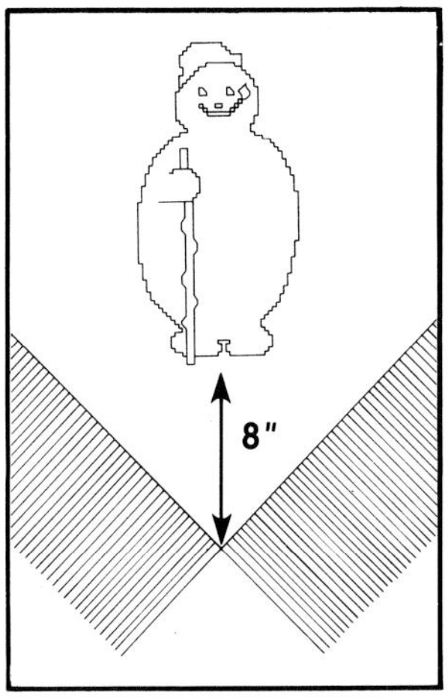

the many faces of santa

X	DMC	¼X	½X	B'ST
	blanc	✓		
	300			
	310			✓
	312			
	321			✓
	322			
	336	✓		
S	356			
+	400			
C	434			
V	498			
	535			
	640			✓
	642			
	644	✓		
	645	✓		✓
	647			
	648	✓		
-	666			
	725			
	754	✓		
X	758	✓		
2	760			
	780			
	781			
	782			
X	783			
	814			
	822	✓		
	838			
	839			
	840			
	926		✓	
	930			
	948			
+	962			
-	3041			
	3064	✓		
X	3072			
	3345			
	3346			
	3347			
	3712	✓		
	3740			
	*781 & gold metallic			
	*783 & gold metallic			
•	310 French Knot			

*Use one strand of gold metallic and two strands of floss.

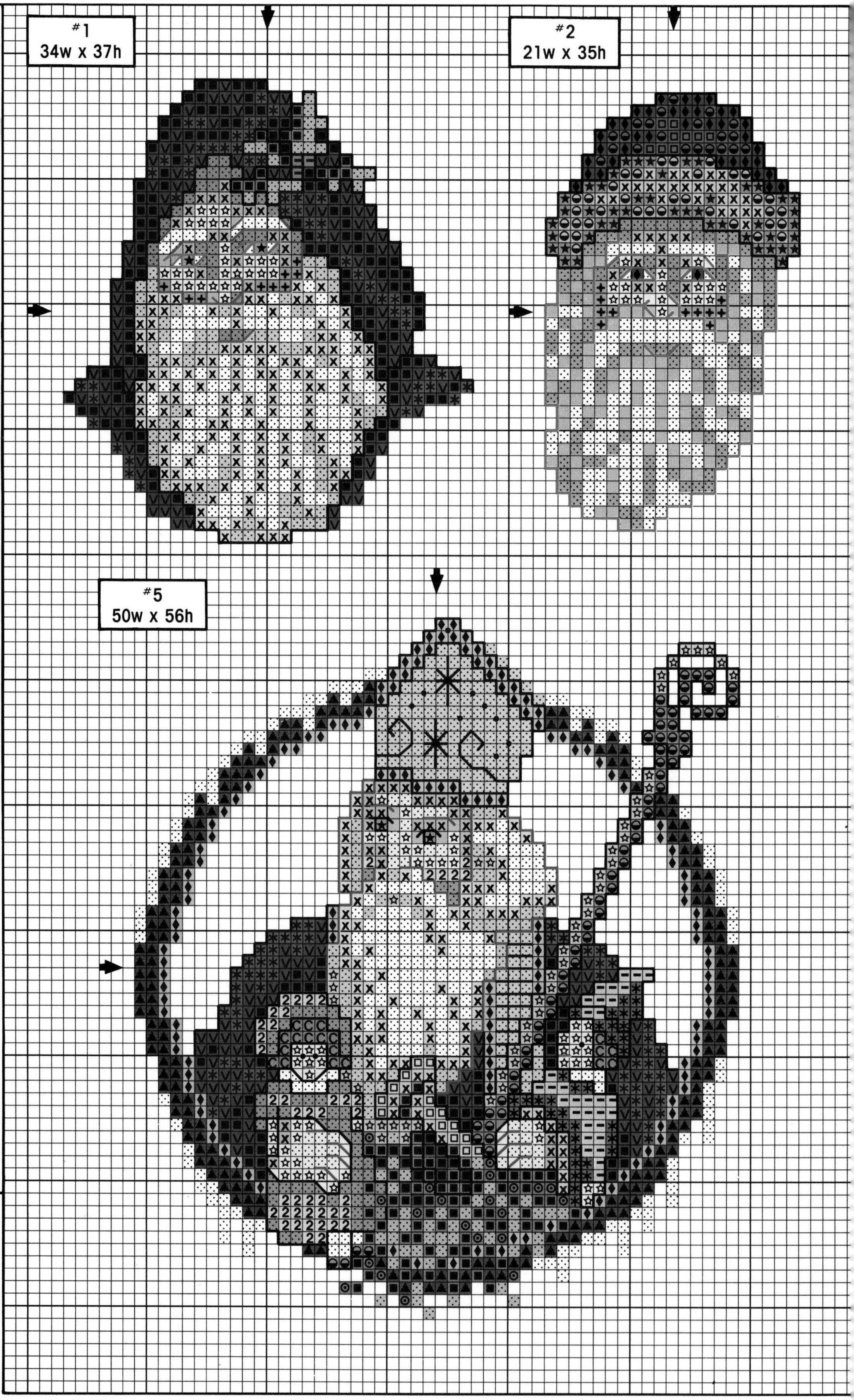

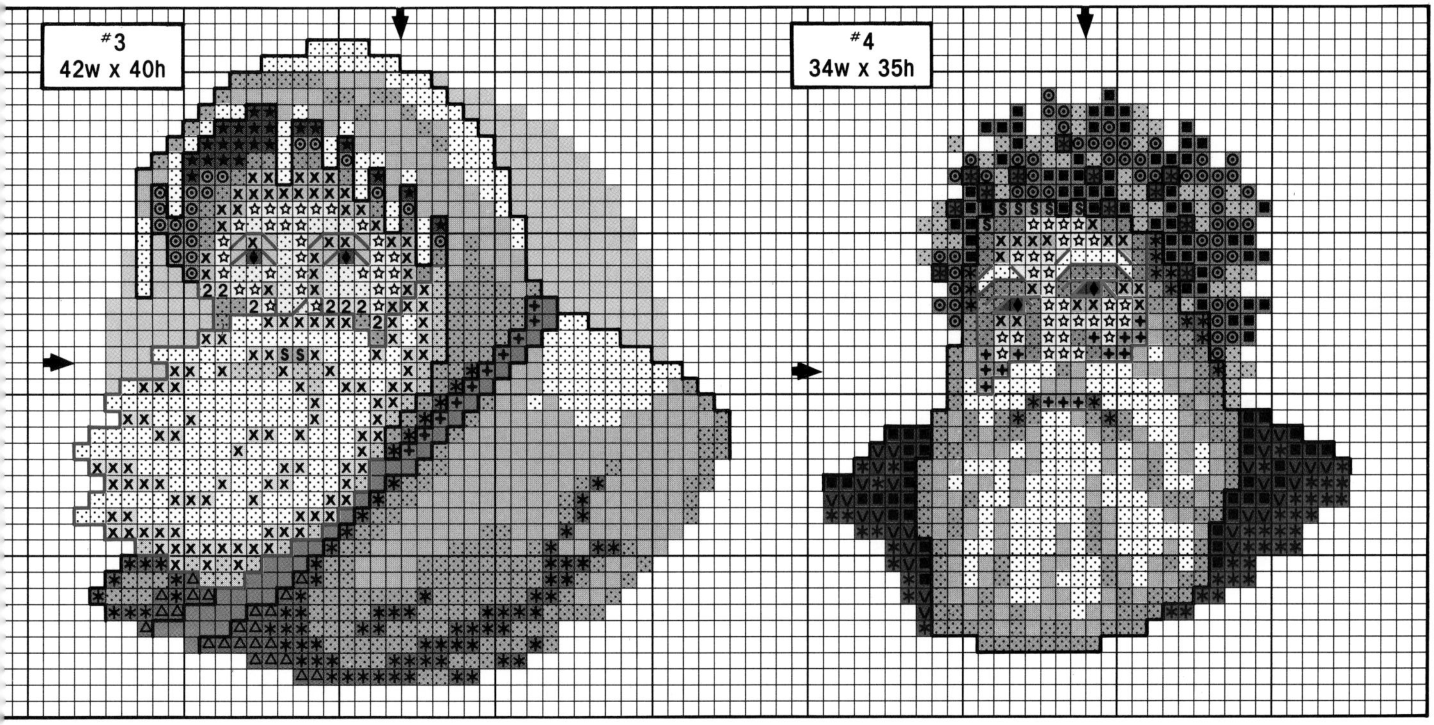

Shown on page 18

Corded Ornaments: Designs #1, #2, and #4 were stitched over 2 fabric threads on 5" squares of Cream Belfast Linen (32 ct). Two strands of floss were used for Cross Stitch and 1 strand for Backstitch.

For each ornament, trim stitched piece 1¼" larger than design on all sides. Cut a piece of Belfast Linen the same size as stitched piece for backing. Matching right sides and raw edges, pin stitched piece and backing fabric together. Using a ½" seam allowance, sew pieces together leaving an opening for turning; clip seam allowance at corners. Turn ornament right side out, carefully pushing corners outward. Stuff ornament with polyester fiberfill and sew final closure by hand.

For twisted cord around each ornament, cut four 60" lengths of six-strand white floss and four 60" lengths of gold braid. Divide lengths into 2 groups with each group containing 2 lengths of floss and 2 lengths of braid. Form 2 loops by folding each group of 4 lengths in half; knot all ends together. Person A holds knotted ends firmly (**Fig. 1**). Counting the number of turns, Person B twists Loop 1 **clockwise** until loop is tight on finger. Hold Loop 1 tightly in free hand. Twisting same number of turns, repeat for Loop 2. Person B places both loops on same finger and twists them together **counterclockwise** one-half the original number of turns (**Fig. 2**), and knots 1" from ends to secure. Beginning and ending at bottom center of ornament, tack twisted cord around edges of ornament.

For each hanger, cut three 39" lengths of six-strand white floss and one 39" length of gold braid. Divide lengths into 2 groups with 1 group containing 2 lengths of white floss and the other group containing 1 length of white floss and 1 length of gold braid. Referring to previous instructions, twist cord. Whipstitch ends of hanger to top corners of ornament.

Fig. 1

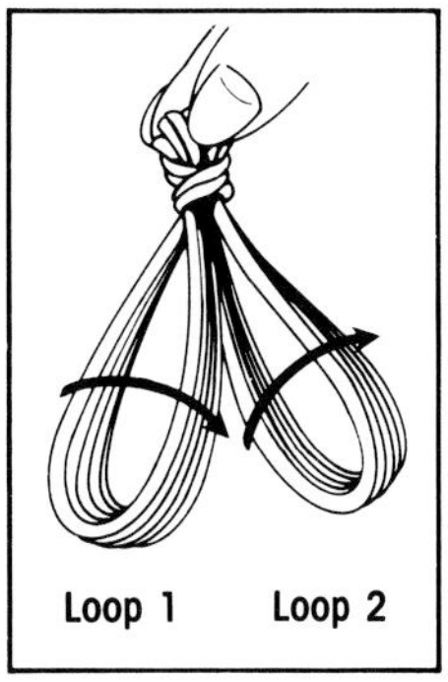

Fig. 2

Gold Frame Ornament: Design #4 was stitched on a 7" square of Raspberry Davosa (18 ct). Two strands of floss were used for Cross Stitch and 1 strand for Backstitch. It was inserted in a 3" dia. gold frame (2⅞" dia. opening).

Hinged Box: Design #5 was stitched over 2 fabric threads on a 9" square of Natural Irish Linen (28 ct). Two strands of floss were used for Cross Stitch and 1 strand for all other stitches. It was inserted in a hinged box (5" square opening).

Pillow: Design #5 was stitched over 2 fabric threads on a 15" square of Victorian Christmas Green Lugana (25 ct). Three strands of floss were used for Cross Stitch and 1 strand for all other stitches.

For pillow, trim stitched piece 3" larger than design on all sides. Cut a piece of Lugana the same size as stitched piece for backing.

For cording, cut one 2" x 37" bias strip of coordinating fabric. Lay purchased cord along center of strip on wrong side of fabric; matching raw edges, fold strip over cord. Using zipper foot, baste along length of strip close to cord; trim seam allowance to ½". Matching raw edges and beginning at bottom center, pin cording to right side of stitched piece making a ⅜" clip in seam allowance of cording at each corner. Ends of cording should overlap approximately 2"; pin overlapping end out of the way. Starting 2" from beginning end of cording and ending 4" from overlapping end, baste cording to stitched piece. On overlapping end of cording, remove 2½" of basting; fold end of fabric back and trim cord so that it meets beginning end of cord. Fold end of fabric under ½"; wrap fabric over beginning end of cording. Finish basting cording to stitched piece.

With right sides facing and leaving an opening for turning, use a ½" seam allowance to sew stitched piece and backing fabric together; clip seam allowance at corners. Turn pillow right side out, carefully pushing corners outward. Stuff pillow with polyester fiberfill and sew final closure by hand.

Porcelain Jar: Design #3 was stitched over 2 fabric threads on an 8" square of Raw Belfast Linen (32 ct). Two strands of floss were used for Cross Stitch and 1 strand for Backstitch. It was inserted in the lid of a 5" dia. porcelain jar (3½" dia. lid opening).

Sweater: Design #1 was stitched over a 9" square of waste canvas (8.5 ct) on a purchased sweater with the top of the design placed 2¼" below bottom of neckband. Six strands of floss were used for Cross Stitch and 2 strands for Backstitch. (See Working on Waste Canvas, page 94.)

Tie: Design #2 was stitched over a 3" x 4" piece of waste canvas (16 ct) on a purchased tie. Three strands of floss were used for Cross Stitch and 1 strand for Backstitch. (See Working on Waste Canvas, page 94.)

shepherds abiding

X	DMC	1/4X	1/2X	B'ST
⁚	blanc	■		
◐	221	■		
★	319			
×	320	■		
	356			■
N	367	■	■	
I	368	■		
Δ	420	■		
C	422	■		
■	550			
V	640		■	■
✱	642	■	■	
I	644		■	
◇	754	■		
◐	758	■		
⁚	760	■		
2	822	■		
■	838		★	
s	839		s	
⁚	869	■		■
▶	890			
⁚	902	■		■
◐	930		■	
□	931		◇	
×	932			
⁚	3031	■		
s	3041			
×	3042			
☆	3045	■		
⁚	3046	■		■
×	3047			
◆	3064	■		
◎	3328			
	3371		■	■
▶	3712			
☆	3721	■		
■	3750		■	
⁚	3779	■		
★	3781	■		
◎	3790			

Grey area indicates last row of top section of design.

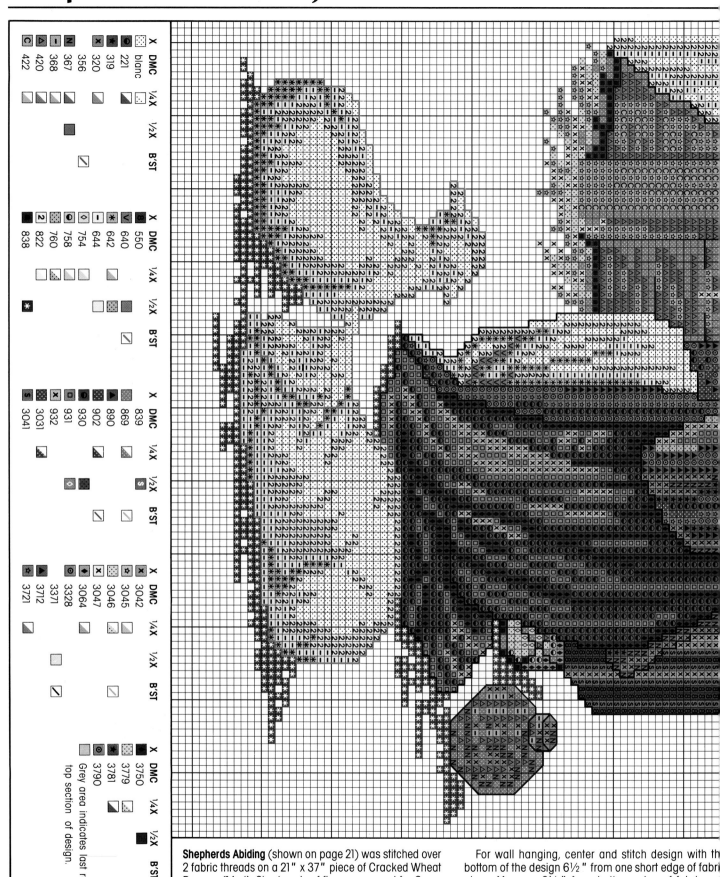

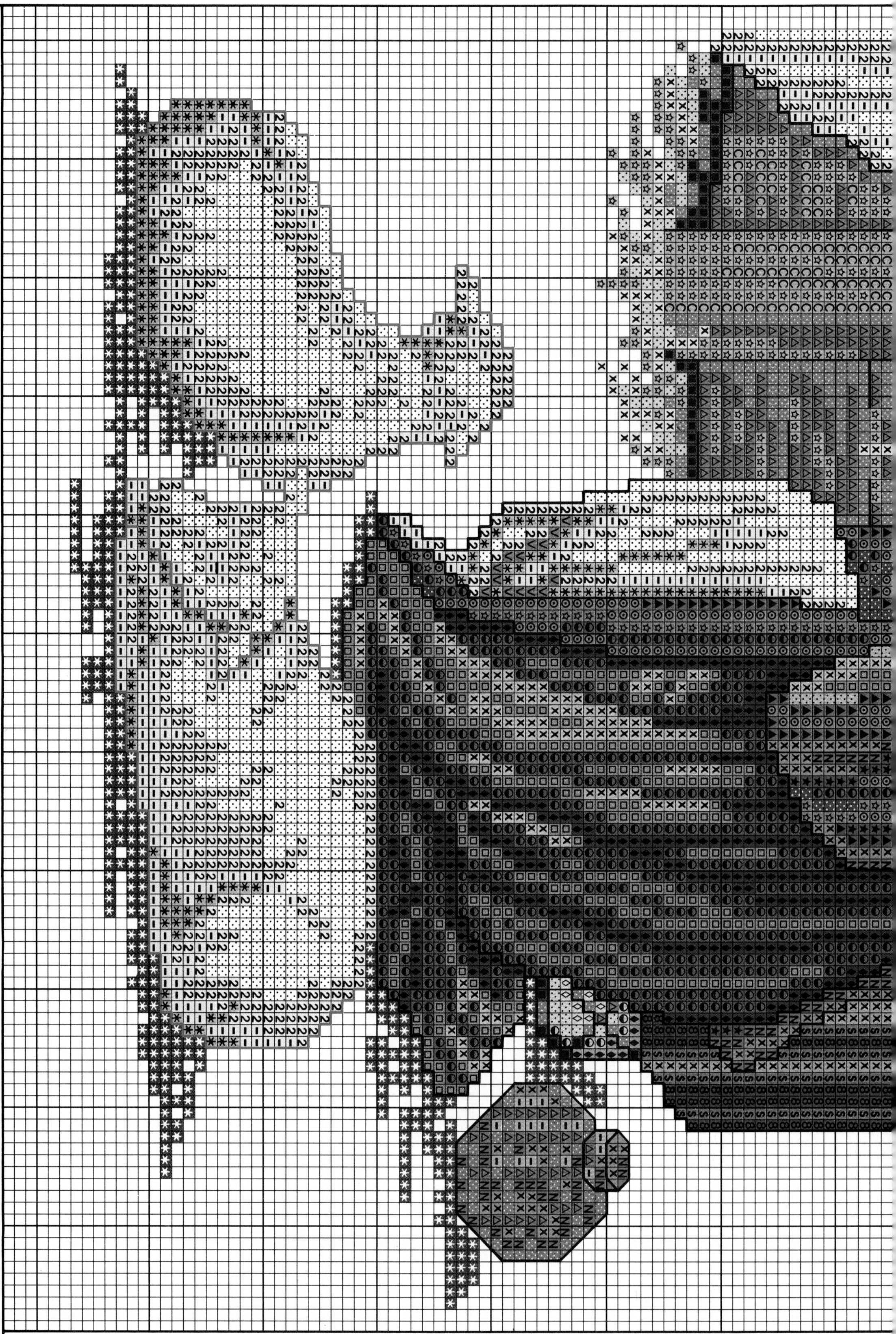

Shepherds Abiding (shown on page 21) was stitched over 2 fabric threads on a 21" x 37" piece of Cracked Wheat Ragusa (14 ct). Six strands of floss were used for Cross Stitch, 1 strand for Half Cross Stitch, and 2 strands for Backstitch. It was made into a wall hanging.

For wall hanging, center and stitch design with the bottom of the design 6½" from one short edge of fabric piece. Measure 3½" from bottom edge of fabric and pull out one fabric thread. Fringe up to missing fabric thread. On each side, turn fabric under ½" and press

urn fabric under ½" again and hem. For casing at top edge, turn fabric under 1" and press; turn fabric under 3" and hem. Insert stick in casing.

108w x 166h
Ye shall find the babe wrapped in swaddling clothes, lying in a manger,
LUKE 2:12

noble companions

DMC	¼X	½X	B'ST
blanc	✓	✓	
319	✓		
321			
349			
351			
420	✓		
422	✓		
498			
640		✓	✓
642			
644			
754	✓		
758	✓		
814	✓		
817			
822			
890	✓		
924	✓		
926	✓		
962			✓
3031	✓		
3032	✓		
3033	✓		
3064	✓		
3345	✓		
3346	✓		
3347			
3371	✓		✓
3768	✓		
3779	✓		
3781	✓		✓
3782	✓		
3790	✓		
gold metallic	✓		✓

Pink area indicates last row of top section of design.

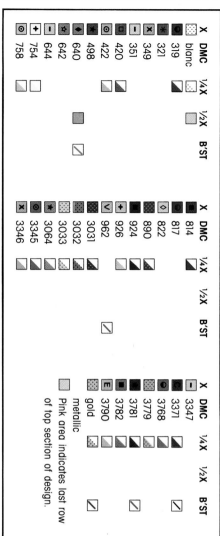

Noble Companions (shown on page 22) was stitched over 2 fabric threads on a 16" x 19" piece of Tea-Dyed Irish Linen (28 ct). Three strands of floss were used for Cross Stitch and 1 strand for all other stitches. It was custom framed.

Santa only (shown on page 23) was stitched on a 9" x 13" piece of Dirty Aida (14 ct). Referring to Arm chart, match **x**'s and ●'s to align arm to Santa's body. **To ensure proper placement of arm on Santa, stitch arm first.** Two strands of floss were used for Cross Stitch and 1 strand for Backstitch. It was made into a stuffed shape.

For stuffed shape, cut stitched piece 1" larger than design on all sides. Cut a piece of Dirty Aida same size as stitched piece for backing.

Matching right sides and raw edges, sew stitched piece and backing fabric together ¼" from design as shown on Diagram, page 95. Leaving a ¼" seam allowance, cut out shape. Clip seam allowance at curves. Turn shape right side out, carefully pushing curves outward.

Baste ½" from raw edge of opening. Stuff shape with polyester fiberfill up to 2" from opening. To weight bottom, fill a plastic sandwich bag with ½ cup aquarium gravel. Place bag into bottom opening of shape.

For base, cut a 6" square of Dirty Aida. Trace base pattern, page 95, onto tracing paper; cut out pattern. Pin pattern to Aida, cut out base. Baste around base ½" from raw edge; press raw edge to wrong side along basting line.

Pull basting thread around opening in shape, drawing up gathers so that opening is slightly smaller than base piece. Pin wrong side of base piece over opening in shape. Whipstitch in place, adding fiberfill as necessary to fill bottom of shape.

STITCH COUNT (101w x 152h)			
Aida 11	9¼"	x	13⅞"
Aida 14	7¼"	x	10⅞"
Linen 28 over 2	7¼"	x	10⅞"
Aida 18	5⅝"	x	8½"
Hardanger 22	4⅝"	x	7"

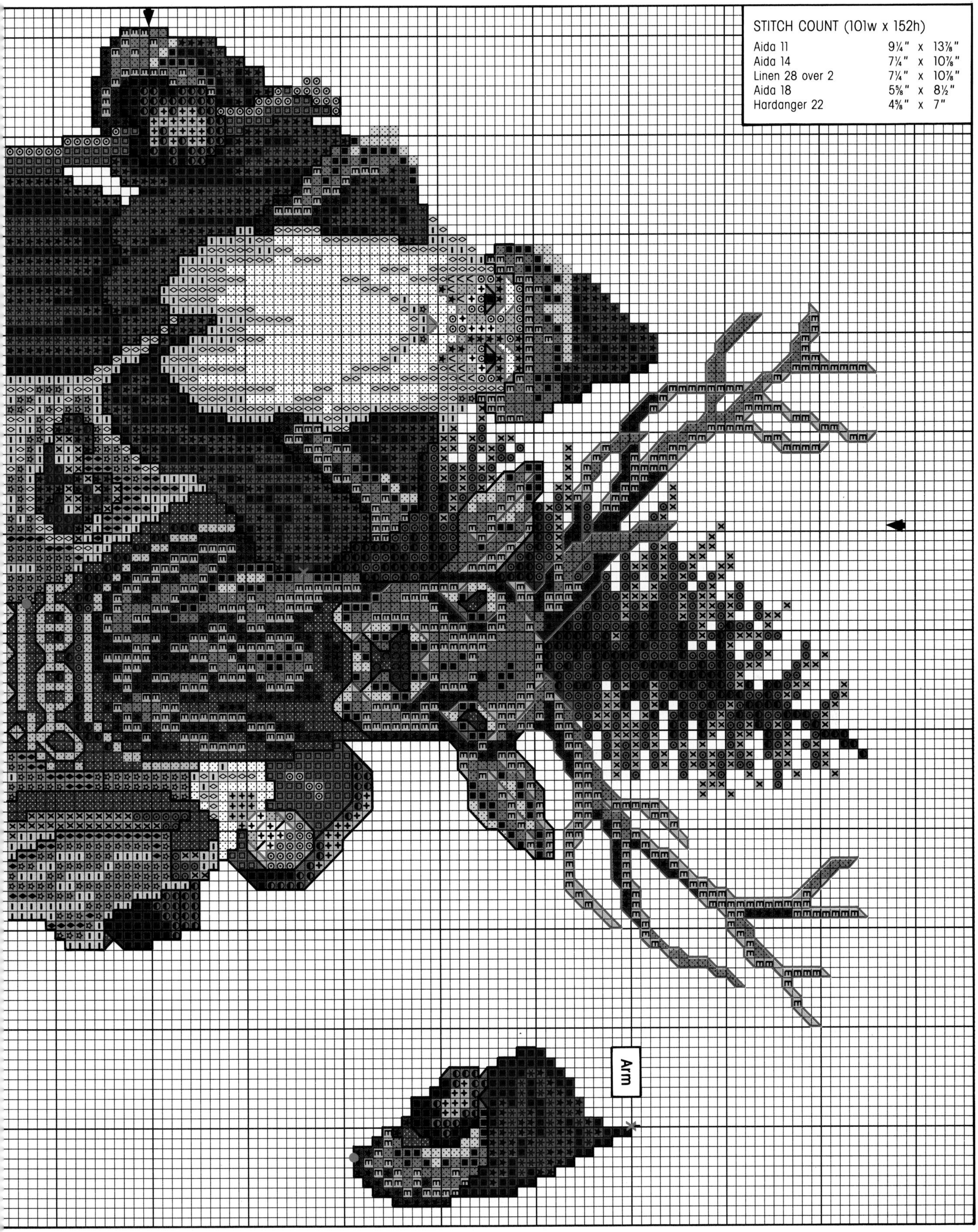

a christmas dream

X	DMC	¼X	½X	B'ST
⋯	blanc	⋯	□	
	221		■	
▣	223		■	✓
◆	319			
◎	320			
◐	353			
■	367		■	
+	368		■	
X	420	✓	◇	
S	422		□	
■	610	✓		
■	640	✓	■	✓
I	642	✓	+	
▣	644		■	
◇	726			
A	727			
N	754	✓	×	
C	758	✓	◎	
I	761			
■	780		■	
▣	782			
+	783		I	
◐	801			
▷	822	✓	×	
	839		◆	✓
◆	869		S	✓
	902		*	
	926		■	
N	927		□	
C	928	✓		
◎	948			
X	963			
⋯	3045	✓	▷	✓
V	3046			
O	3078			
■	3712	✓		
▶	3722		×	
	3768		V	
⋯	3773	✓	N	
8	3779	✓		

Pink line indicates last row of top section of design.

STITCH COUNT (104w x 154h)

Aida 11	9½" x 14"
Aida 14	7½" x 11"
Linen 32 over 2	6½" x 9⅝"
Aida 18	5⅞" x 8⅝"
Hardanger 22	4¾" x 7"

A Christmas Dream (shown on page 25) was stitched over 2 fabric threads on a 15" x 18" piece of Cream Belfast Linen (32 ct). Two strands of floss were used for Cross Stitch and 1 strand for all other stitches. It was custom framed.

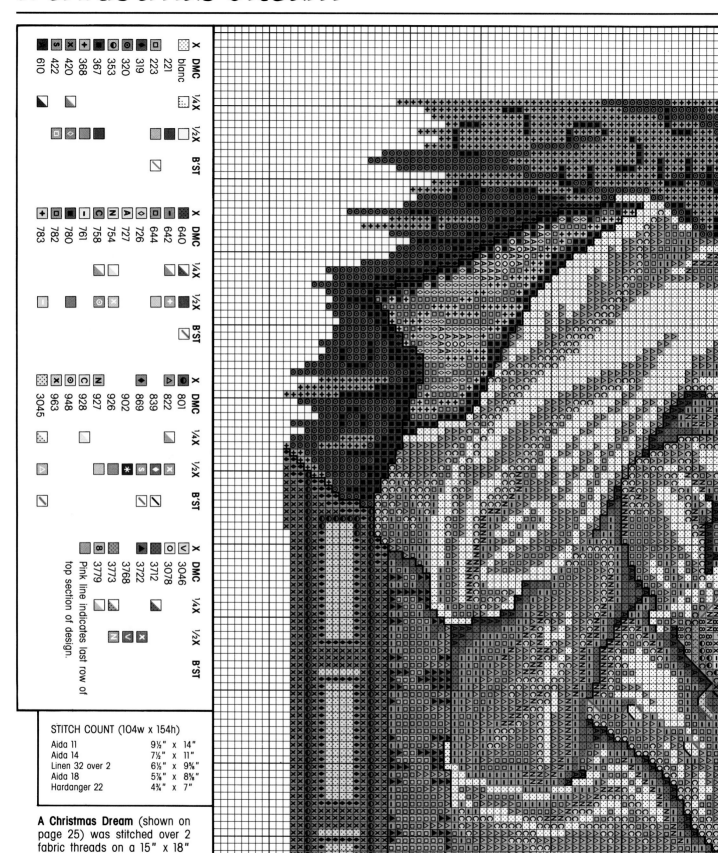

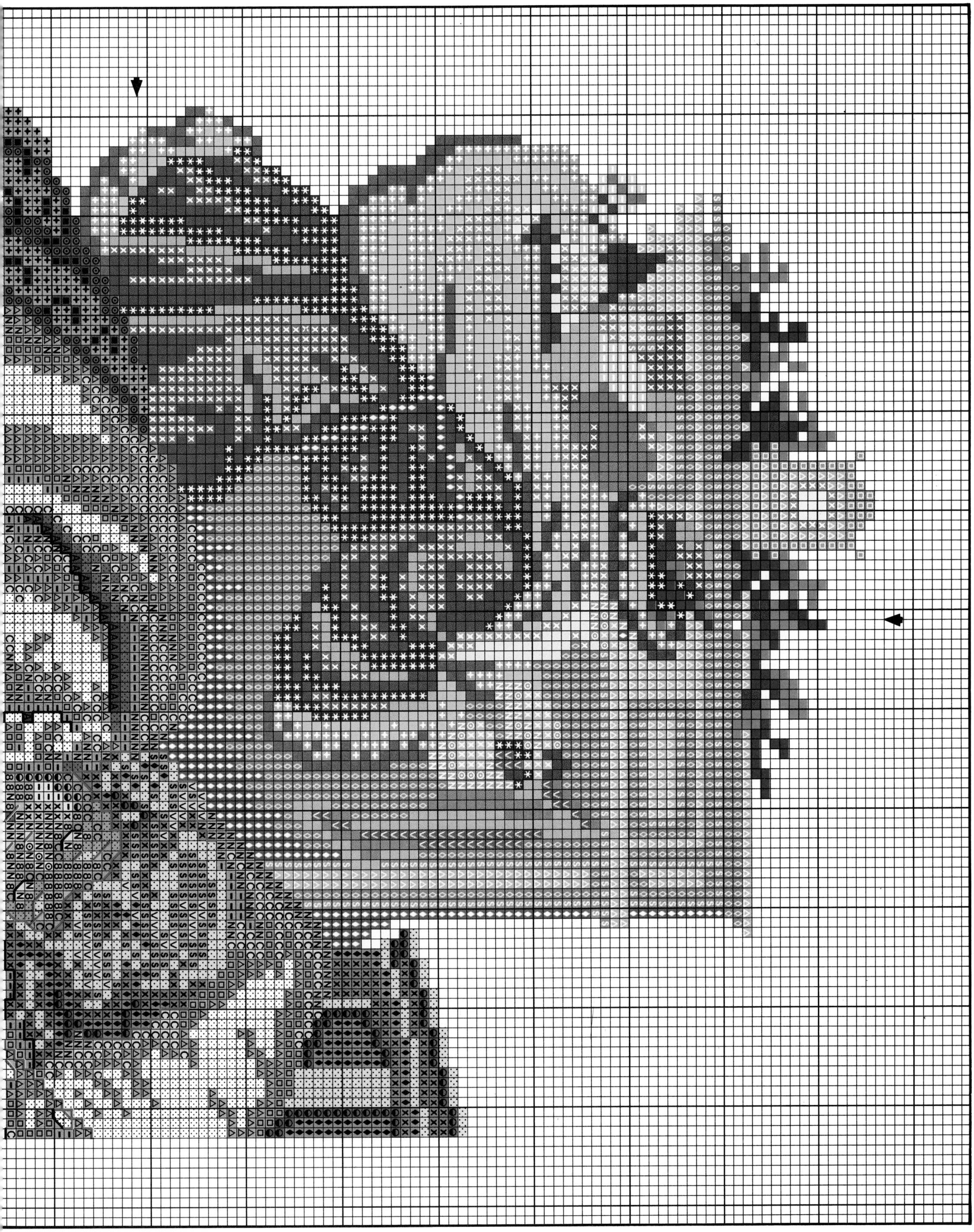

earth angels

Earth Angels (shown on page 26) were each stitched over 2 fabric threads on a 9" x 12" piece of Cream Belfast Linen (32 ct). Two strands of floss were used for Cross Stitch and 1 strand for all other stitches except as indicated in color key. They were made into hanging pillows.

For each pillow, trace pattern onto tracing paper; cut out pattern. Center pattern on wrong side of stitched piece with top of pattern 1½" above star at top of design. Draw around pattern with fabric marking pencil. Leaving ½" seam allowance on all sides, cut out pillow. Cut a piece of Belfast Linen the same size as stitched piece for backing.

For gold cording, cut one 2" x 30" bias strip of gold lamé. Center cording on wrong side of bias strip; matching long edges, fold strip over cord. Using zipper foot, baste along length of strip close to cord; trim seam allowance to ½". Matching raw edges and beginning on one side, pin cording to right side of stitched piece, making a ⅜" clip in seam allowance of cording at each corner. Ends of cording should overlap approximately 2"; pin overlapping end out of the way. Starting 2" from beginning end of cording and ending 4" from overlapping end, sew cording to stitched piece. On overlapping end of cording, remove 2½" of basting; fold end of fabric back and trim cord so it meets beginning end of cord. Fold end of fabric under ½"; wrap fabric over beginning end of cording. Finish sewing cording to stitched piece.

For fabric cording, cut one 2½" x 30" bias strip of fabric. Lay purchased cord along center of strip on wrong side of fabric; matching long edges, fold strip over cord. Using zipper foot, baste along length of strip close to cord; trim seam allowance to ¾". Repeat above instructions to sew cording to stitched piece.

With right sides facing and leaving an opening for turning, use a ½" seam allowance to sew stitched piece and backing fabric together; trim seam allowances diagonally at corners. Turn pillow right side out, carefully pushing corners outward. Stuff pillow with polyester fiberfill and sew final closure by hand.

For tassel, cut 6 yd lengths **each** of ecru and green six-strand embroidery floss and gold metallic thread. Wind the three lengths approximately 35 times around a 3" square piece of cardboard. Cut an 8" length of green embroidery floss and insert under all strands at one end of cardboard; pull tightly and tie securely (**Fig. 1**). Cut floss and thread at opposite end of cardboard. Do not trim 8" length of floss.

Fig. 1

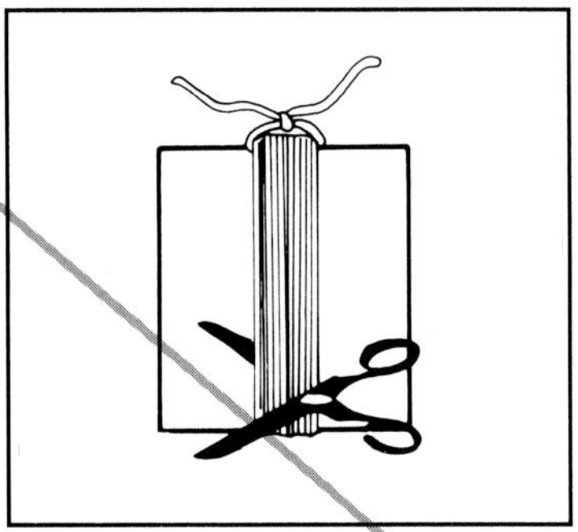

To wrap tassel, cut an 18" length of green embroidery floss. Make a 3" loop at one end of the length; lay loop on tassel as shown in **Fig. 2**. Beginning ¾" from top of tassel and holding loop in place, tightly wrap remainder of length around tassel 6 times (**Fig. 3**).

Fig. 2

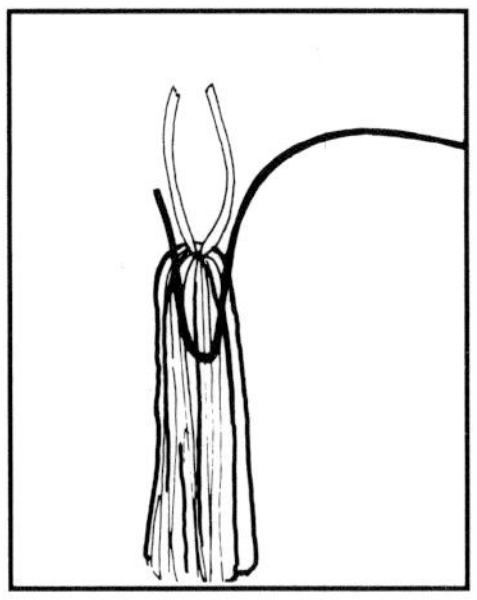

Fig. 3

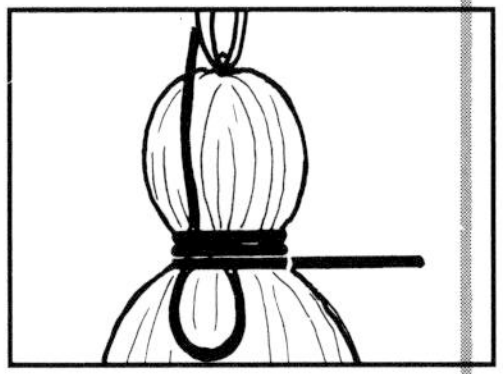

Place end of length through loop (**Fig. 4**). Pull other end of length as indicated by arrow in **Fig. 4** to conceal loop beneath wrapped area; trim ends.

Fig. 4

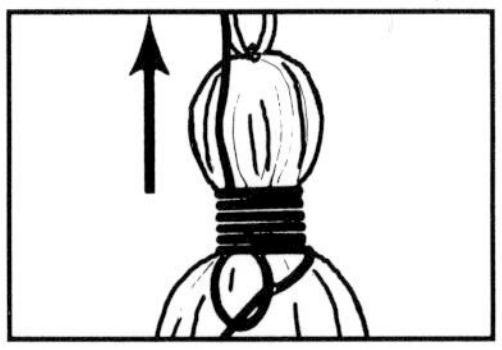

Evenly trim ends of tassel. Whipstitch top of tassel to bottom point of pillow; trim ends of 8" length of floss.

For twisted cord hanger, cut two 63" lengths of six-strand green floss, two 63" lengths of six-strand ecru floss, and two 63" lengths of fine gold braid. Divide lengths into 2 groups with each group containing 1 length of green floss, 1 length of ecru floss, and 1 length of braid. Form 2 loops by folding each group of 3 lengths in half; knot all ends together 1" from ends. Person A holds knotted ends firmly (**Fig. 5**). Counting the number of turns, Person B twists Loop 1 **clockwise** until loop is tight on finger. Hold Loop 1 tightly in free hand. Twisting same number of turns, repeat for Loop 2. Person B places both loops on same finger and twists them together **counterclockwise** one-half the original number of turns (**Fig. 6**), and knots 1" from ends to secure. Whipstitch ends of hanger to top corners of pillow.

Fig. 5

Fig. 6

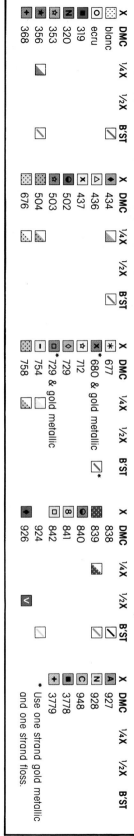

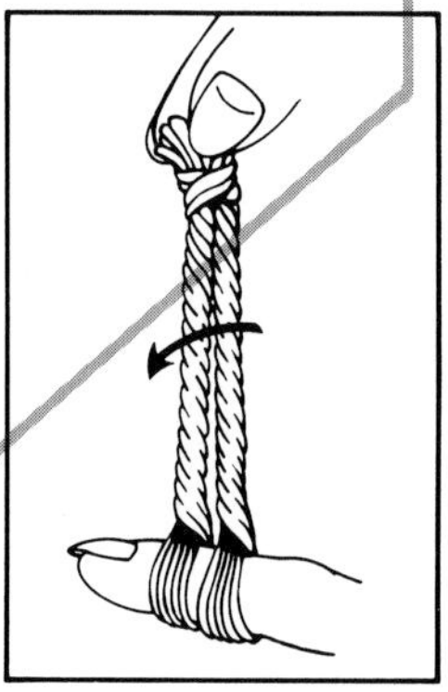

X	DMC	¼X	½X	B'ST
■	blanc			■
■	ecru			
■	319			
■	320			
■	353			
■	356	■		■
■	368			
■	434	■		■
■	436			
■	437			
■	502			
■	503			
■	504	■		
■	676	■		
■	677			
■	*680 & gold metallic			■*
■	712			
■	729			
■	*729 & gold metallic	■		
■	754			
■	758	■		
■	838			■
■	839	■		■
■	840			
■	841			
■	842			
	924			■
■	926		■	
■	927			
■	928			
■	948			
■	3778			
■	3779			

* Use one strand gold metallic and one strand floss.

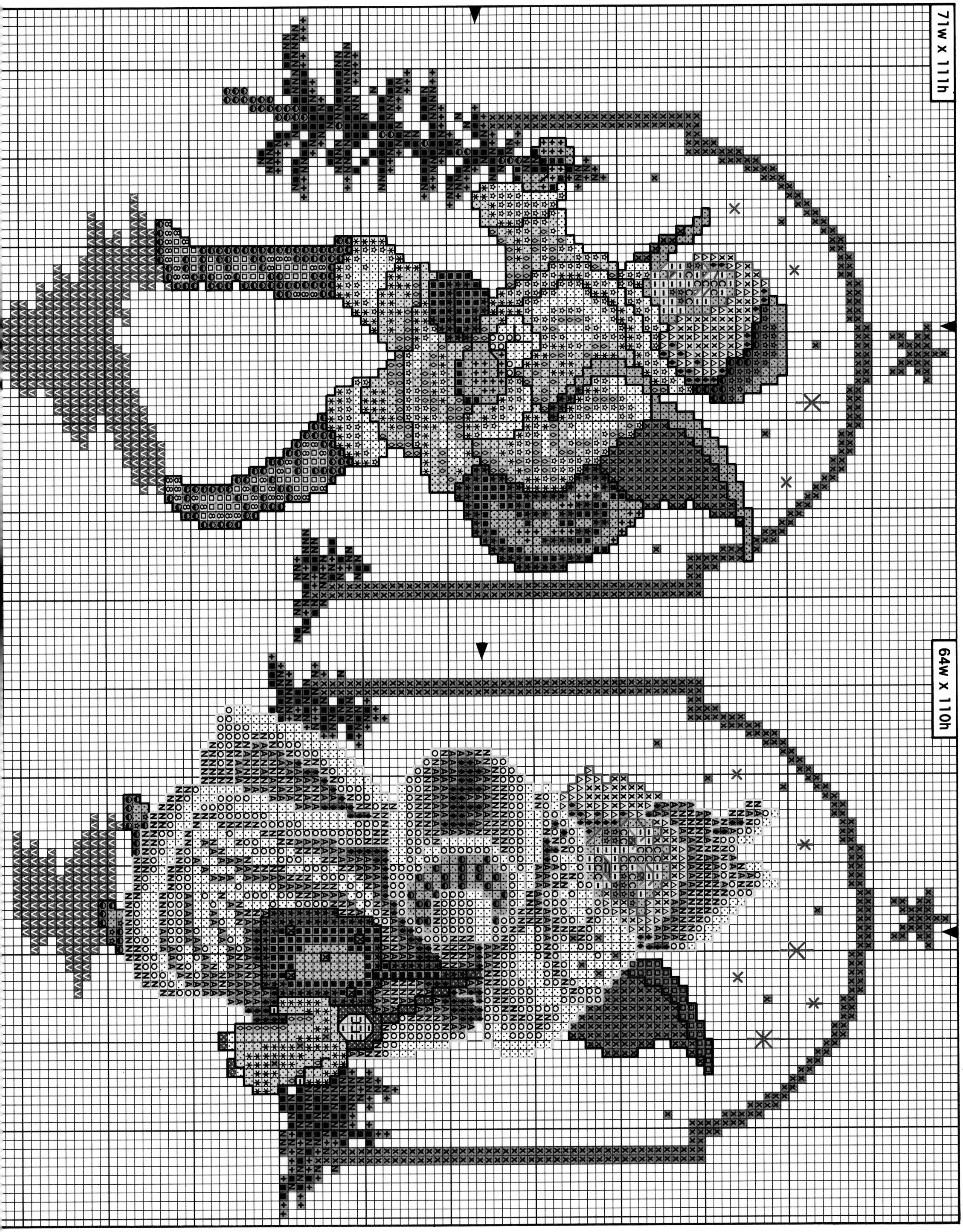
71w x 111h
64w x 110h

OLDE WORLD TRAVELER

X	DMC	¼X	½X	B'ST
■	blanc	■	■	
■	223			
■	224			
■	225			
■	326			
■	535	■		
■	611	■		
■	612			
■	613			
■	640		■	■
■	642	■	■	
■	644	■		
■	676	■		
■	677	■		
■	680	■		
■	729	■		
■	754	■		
■	758	■		
■	780	■		
■	781			
■	815	■		■
■	822	■		
■	838	■		
■	839			
■	840			
■	841			
■	842			
■	902	■		
■	931	■		
■	962			
■	3041			
■	3042			
■	3051			
■	3052			
■	3053	■		
■	3064	■		
■	3345	■		
■	3346			
■	3347			
	3371			■
■	3722			
■	3740			
■	3743			
■	3779	■		
■	gold metallic			■
■	3371 French Knot			

Blue area indicates last row of top section of design.

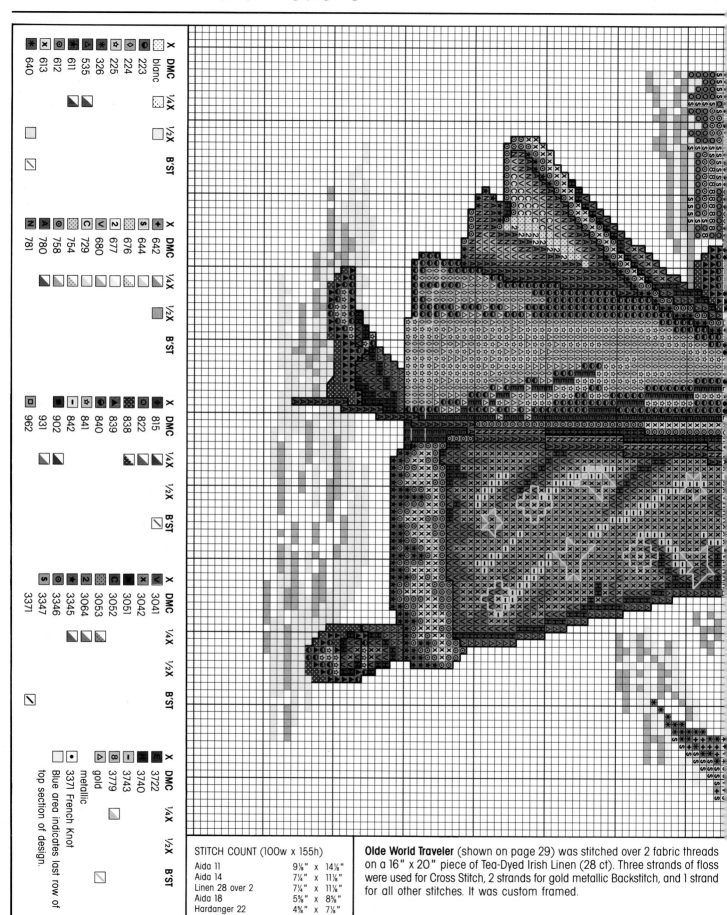

STITCH COUNT (100w x 155h)

Aida 11	9⅛"	x	14⅛"
Aida 14	7¼"	x	11⅛"
Linen 28 over 2	7¼"	x	11⅛"
Aida 18	5⅝"	x	8⅝"
Hardanger 22	4⅝"	x	7⅛"

Olde World Traveler (shown on page 29) was stitched over 2 fabric threads on a 16" x 20" piece of Tea-Dyed Irish Linen (28 ct). Three strands of floss were used for Cross Stitch, 2 strands for gold metallic Backstitch, and 1 strand for all other stitches. It was custom framed.

and to all a good night

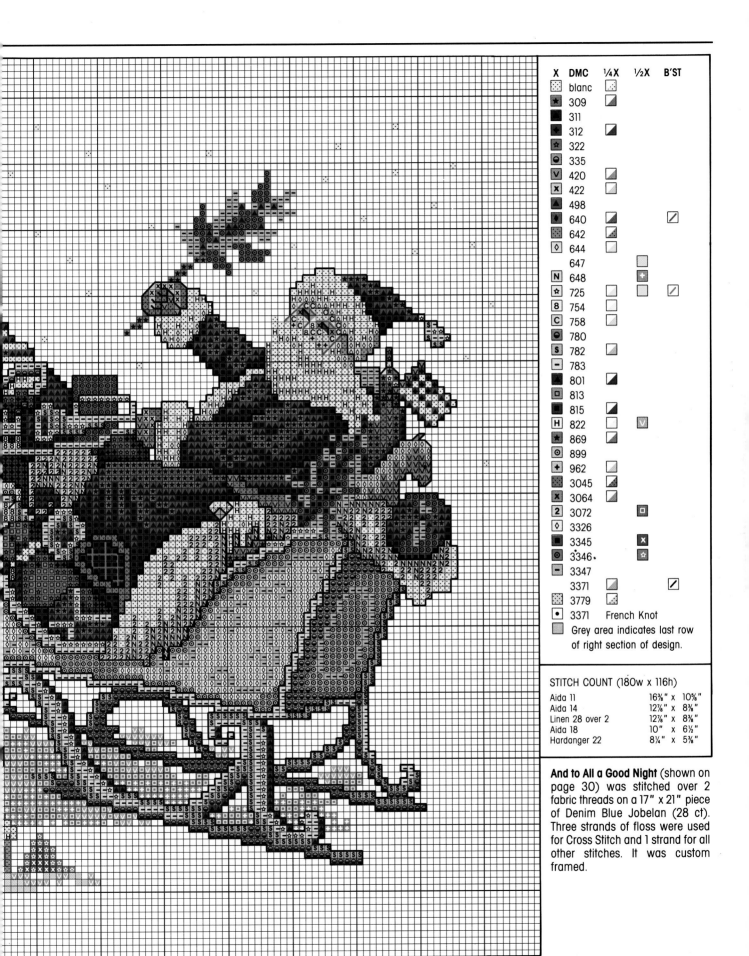

X	DMC	¼X	½X	B'ST
	blanc	■		
	309	■		
	311			
	312	■		
	322			
	335			
V	420	■		
X	422	■		
	498			
	640	■		■
	642	■		
	644	■		
	647		■	
N	648		■	
	725	■	■	■
8	754	■		
C	758	■		
	780			
S	782	■		
–	783			
	801	■		
	813			
	815	■		
H	822	■	■	
	869	■		
	899			
	962	■		
	3045	■		
X	3064	■		
2	3072		■	
	3326			
	3345		■	
	3346		■	
–	3347			
	3371	■		■
	3779	■		
•	3371 French Knot			
	Grey area indicates last row of right section of design.			

STITCH COUNT (180w x 116h)

Aida 11	16⅜"	x	10⅝"
Aida 14	12⅞"	x	8⅜"
Linen 28 over 2	12⅞"	x	8⅜"
Aida 18	10"	x	6½"
Hardanger 22	8¼"	x	5⅜"

And to All a Good Night (shown on page 30) was stitched over 2 fabric threads on a 17" x 21" piece of Denim Blue Jobelan (28 ct). Three strands of floss were used for Cross Stitch and 1 strand for all other stitches. It was custom framed.

children of yesteryear

Children of Yesteryear (shown on page 32) was stitched over 2 fabric threads on an 11" x 12" piece of Cream Belfast Linen (32 ct). Two strands of floss were used for Cross Stitch and 1 strand for all other stitches. It was applied to the front of a fabric covered photo album.

For album, cut one 39" x 13½" piece of fabric to cover a 10"w x 11½"h album with a 2" spine. Cut one 38" x 11½" piece of fusible web and one 38" x 11½" piece of craft batting.

Center web, then batting on wrong side of fabric (**Fig. 1**); follow manufacturer's instructions to fuse batting to fabric. Press short edges of fabric ½" to wrong side (over edges of batting) and glue to batting; allow glue to dry.

To form pockets for album, fold one short edge of fabric approx. 9" to right side; fold remaining short edge 7" to right side (adjust pocket sizes as necessary to fit individual albums). Using a 1" seam allowance, sew across top and bottom of pockets; trim corners. Turn cover right side out. Fold remaining raw edges 1" to wrong side and glue to batting; allow glue to dry. Slip front cover of album into large pocket and back cover into small pocket.

To pad stitched piece, cut a piece of cardboard and a piece of craft batting 6½" x 8". Center batting, then cardboard on wrong side of stitched piece. Fold edges of stitched piece to back of cardboard and glue in place; allow glue to dry.

Cut a 32" length of 1½"w gathered lace. Turn short edges to wrong side ½" and press. Referring to photo and beginning at bottom edge of stitched piece, glue gathered edge of lace to back of stitched piece. Center and glue padded stitched piece to front of album cover; allow glue to dry.

Cut a 50" length of ¼" dia cord. Starting 8" from one end of cord, refer to **Fig. 2** and lay cord around edge of padded stitched piece, beginning and ending at left side. Glue cord in place; allow glue to dry. Tie cord in a knot. Tie each end of cord in a knot; trim ends.

Fig. 1

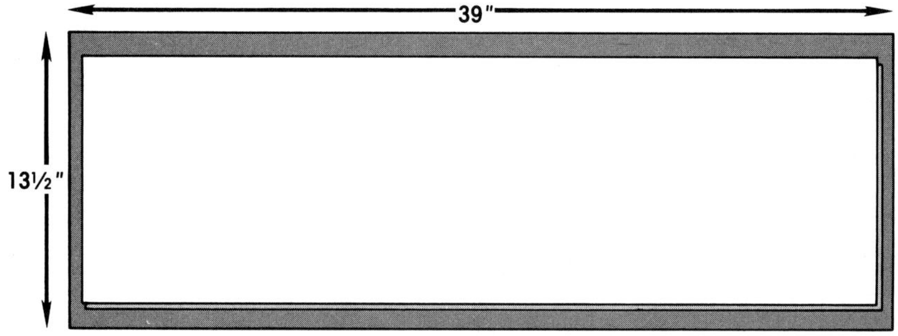

Fig. 2

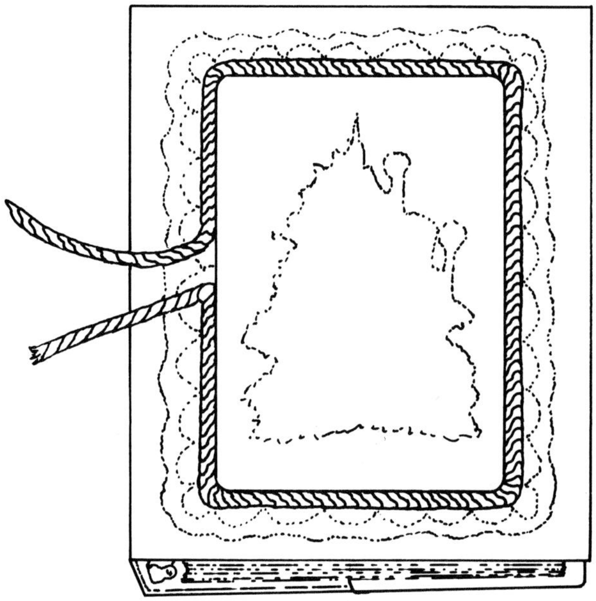

X	DMC	¼X	½X	B'ST
⁙	blanc	◩		
✱	321	◩		◩
△	353	◩		
	356			◩
▲	420	◩		
⁙	725	◩	□	
−	726	◩		
8	740	◩		◩
⁙	754	◩		
◒	758	◩		
■	780	◩		
◊	782	◩		
✱	783	◩		
■	814	◩		
◒	815	◩		
×	816	◩		
S	822	◩		
V	839	◩		◩
♦	869	◩		◩
⁙	930	◩		
⊙	931	◩		
+	932	◩		
H	3022	◩		
V	3023	◩		
⁙	3024	◩		
⊙	3045	◩		
+	3046			
C	3047			
♦	3064	◩		
O	3078			
	3328			◩
◒	3345	◩		
◊	3346	◩		
□	3347	◩		
−	3752			
⊙	3779	◩		

77w x 98h

meeting with santa

Meeting with Santa (shown on page 35) was stitched over 2 fabric threads on a 45" x 58" piece of Ivory Anne Cloth (18 ct). It was made into an afghan.

For afghan, cut off selvages of fabric; measure 5½" from raw edge of fabric and pull out 1 fabric thread. Fringe fabric up to missing fabric thread. Repeat for each side. Tie an overhand knot at each corner with 4 horizontal and 4 vertical fabric threads. Working from corners, use 8 fabric threads for each knot until all threads are knotted.

Refer to Diagram for placement of design on fabric; use 6 strands of floss for Cross Stitch and 2 strands for all other stitches.

Diagram

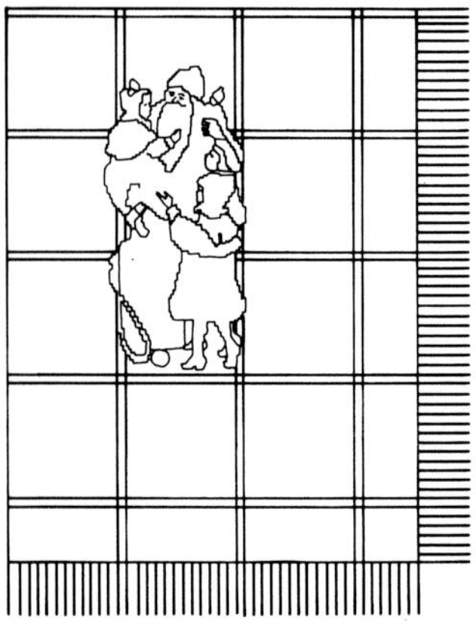

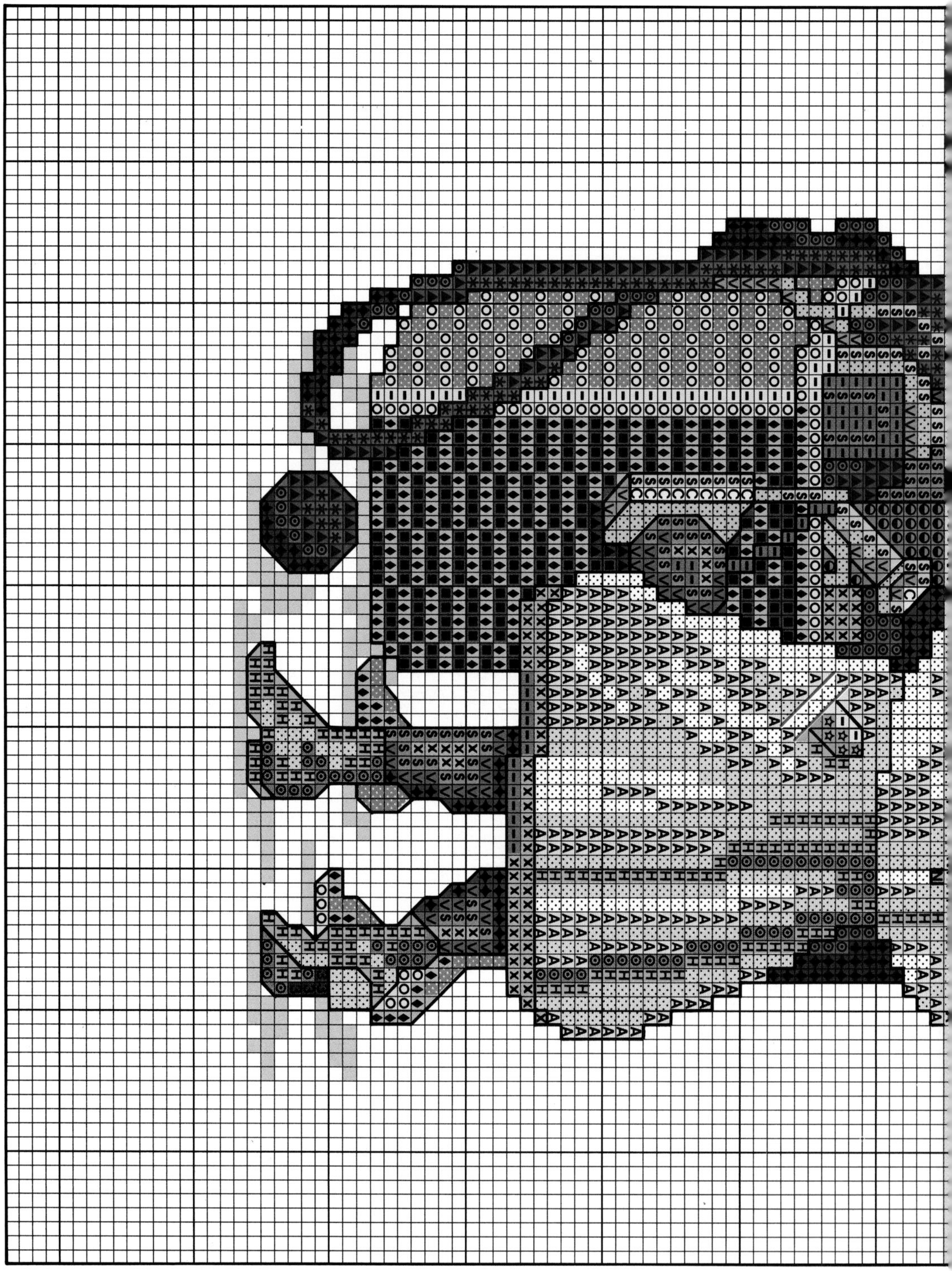

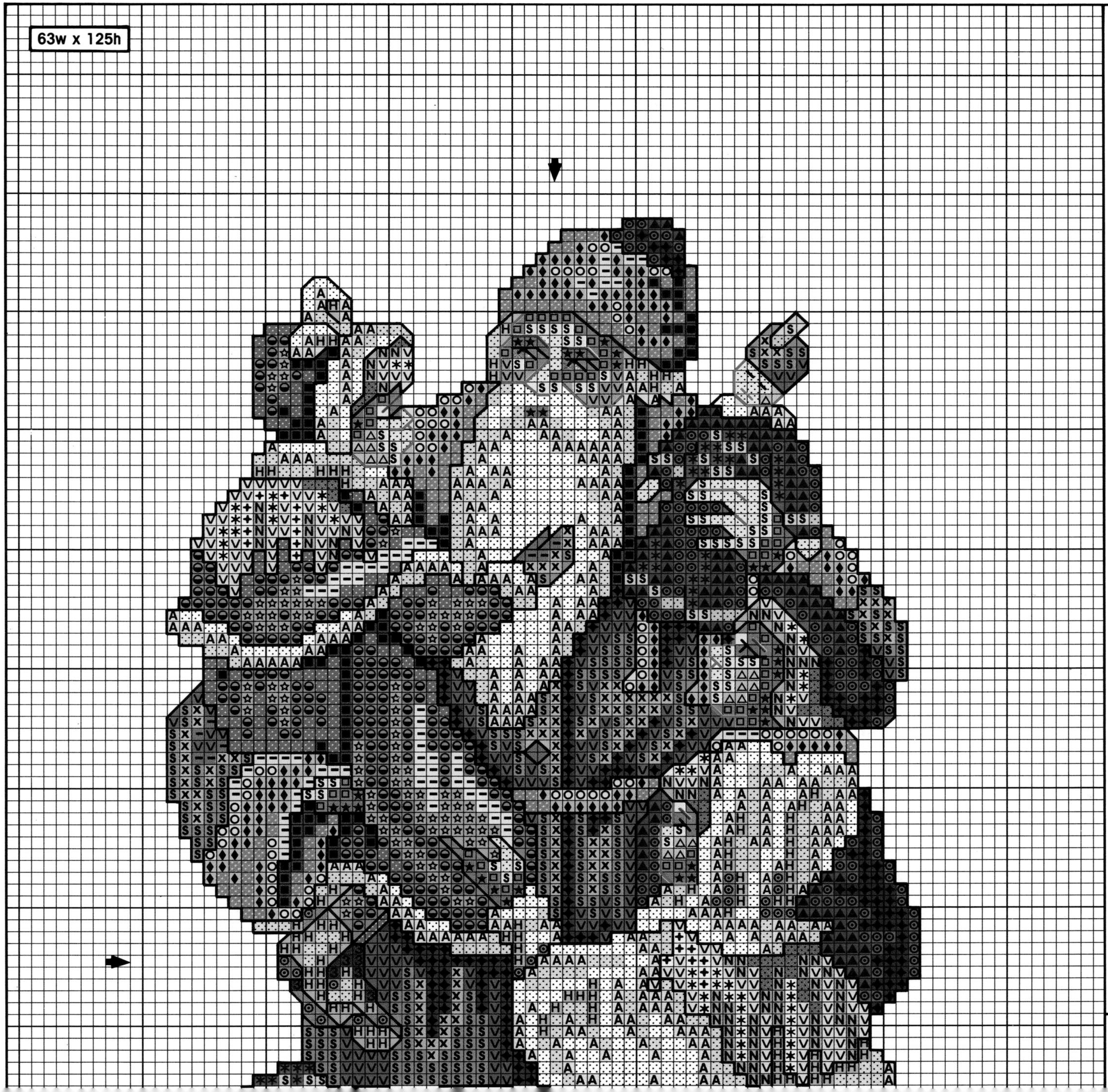

X	DMC	¼X	½X	B'ST
	blanc	◩		
■	319	◩		
◐	320	◩		
✱	321	◩		
◆	336	◩		
△	353	◩		
	356			◩
	367	◩		
☆	368	◩		
−	369	◩		
	420	◩		
▲	498	◩		◩
	610	◩		◩
♦	611	◩		
O	612	◩		
−	613			
⊙	640	◩	◩	◩
H	642	◩		
	644	◩		
✱	676	◩		
+	677			
N	680	◩		
S	725	◩		
C	726	◩		
V	729	◩		
	754	◩		
◻	758	◩		
V	781	◩		
	783	◩		
−	813	◩		
◆	814	◩		
⊙	815	◩		
A	822	◩		
V	824	◩		
S	825	◩		
X	826	◩		
V	962	◩		
★	3064	◩		
▲	3371			◩
S	3779	◩		
■	3781	◩		
	3790	◩		

Pink area indicates last row of top section of design.

X	DMC	¼X	½X	B'ST
⋯	blanc			
O	ecru			
◓	304			
	310			■
✱	321			
C	322	■		
	356			■
	413			■
▲	415			
■	420	■		
S	433	■		
◎	435			
V	470			
◆	498	■		
◊	644			
N	645	■		
R	676			
−	677			
♦	680	■		■
△	729	■		
+	738			
2	739			
✱	746	■		
☆	754	■		
◓	758	■		
△	760	■		
⋯	761	■		
	814			■
	815			■
★	838			■
C	839			
◓	844	■		■
3	927	■		
△	928	■	■	
◘	3023	■		
A	3024	■		
x	3072			
8	3345			
	3787		V	
V*	gold metallic & 729	■		
☆	gold metallic			■ †
●	310 French Knot			
●	815 French Knot			

* Use one strand of gold metallic and two strands of 729.

† Use two strands for harp strings and work in long stitches.

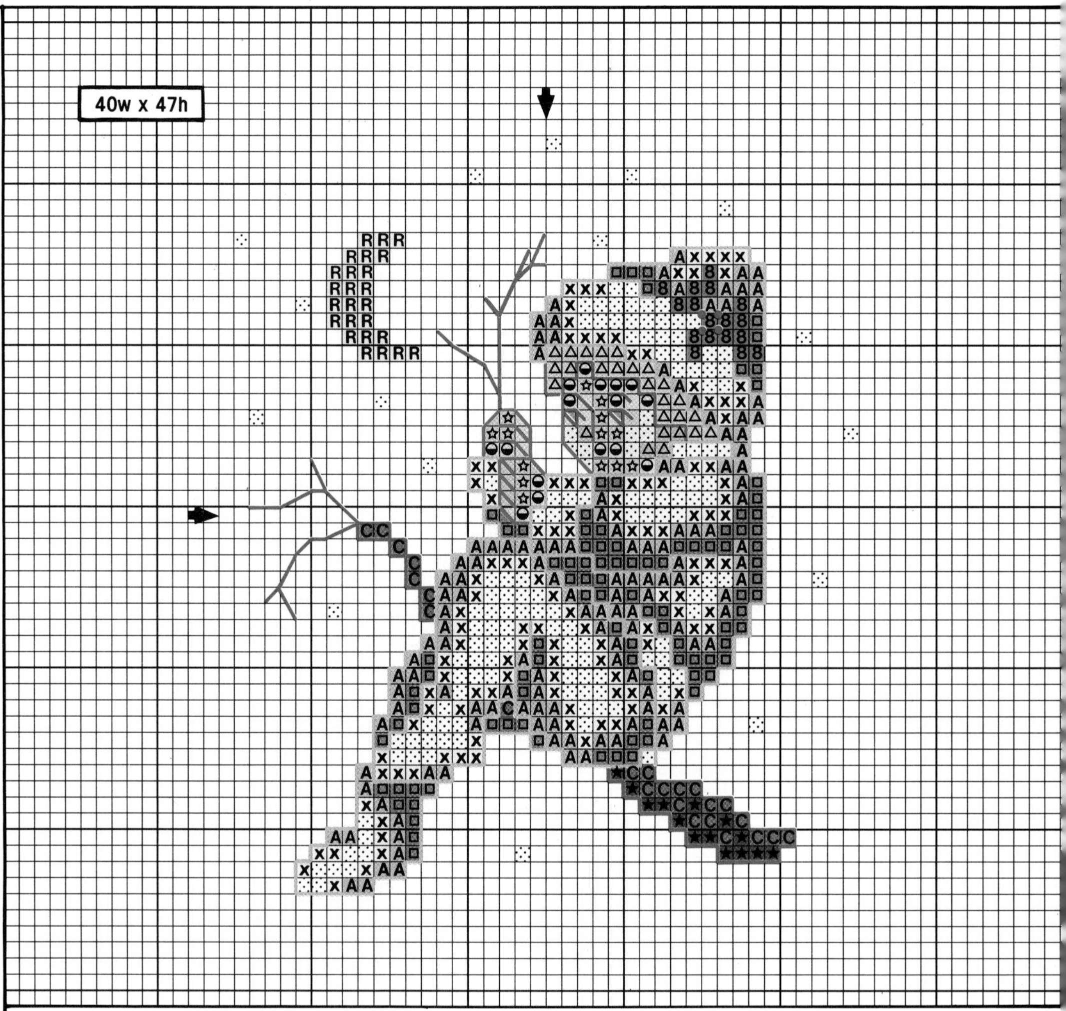

Portraits in Miniature designs (shown on page 36) were each stitched over 2 fabric threads on a 7" square of Raw Belfast Linen (32 ct). Two strands of floss were used for Cross Stitch and 1 strand for all other stitches except as indicated in color key. They were made into hanging ornaments.

For each ornament, trim stitched piece 1" larger than design on all sides. For backing fabric, cut a piece of Raw Belfast Linen the same size as stitched piece. Matching right sides and raw edges, pin stitched piece and backing fabric together. Leaving an opening for turning, use a ½" seam allowance to sew pieces together; trim seam allowance diagonally at corners. Turn ornament right side out, carefully pushing corners outward. Stuff ornament with polyester fiberfill and sew final closure by hand.

For twisted cord around each ornament, use colors of floss to match stitched piece. To find desired length to cut floss, add 5" to outside measurement of ornament and multiply by 3. Using determined measurement, cut two groups of floss, each group containing 3 lengths of six-strand floss. (**Note:** If using gold metallic thread, cut two strands the determined length to use with the other floss colors.) Form 2 loops by folding each group of floss in half; knot all ends together 1" from ends. Person A holds knotted ends firmly (**Fig. 1**). Counting the number of turns, Person B twists Loop 1 **clockwise** until loop is tight on finger. Hold Loop 1 tightly in free hand. Twisting same number of turns, repeat for Loop 2. Person B places both loops on same finger and twists them together **counterclockwise** one-half the original number of turns (**Fig. 2**), and knots 1" from ends to secure. Beginning and ending at bottom center of ornament, start 1¼" from one end of twisted cord and tack twisted cord around edges of ornament. Fold one end of twisted cord over the other end; tack to back of ornament.

For hanger, run a 10" length of nylon line through backing fabric at top center of ornament; knot ends together.

Fig. 1

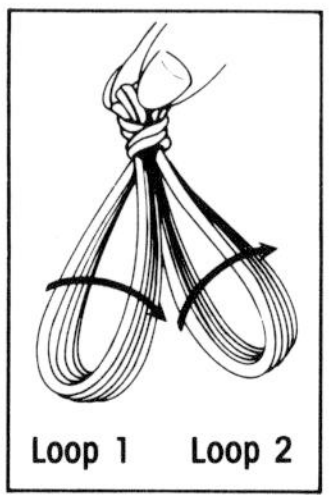

Fig. 2

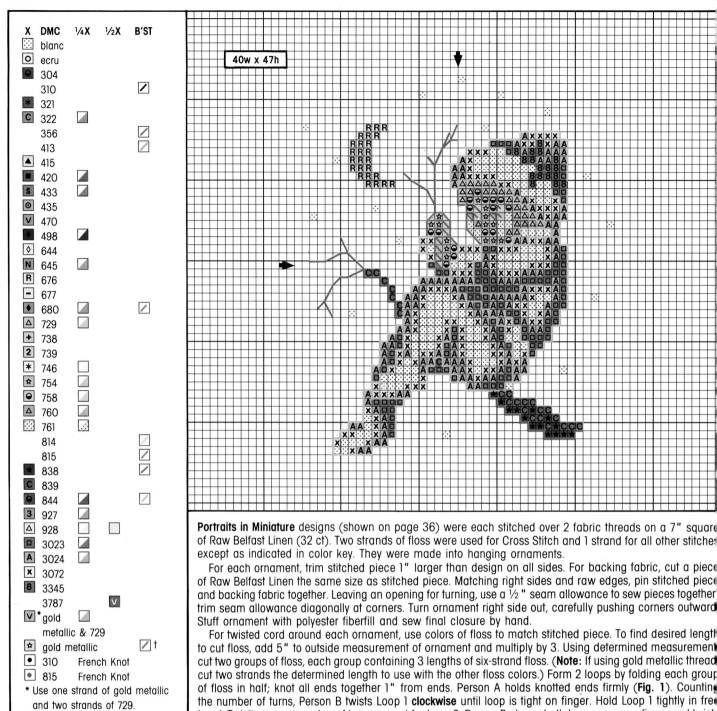

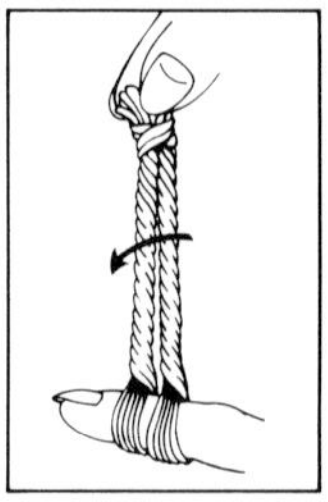

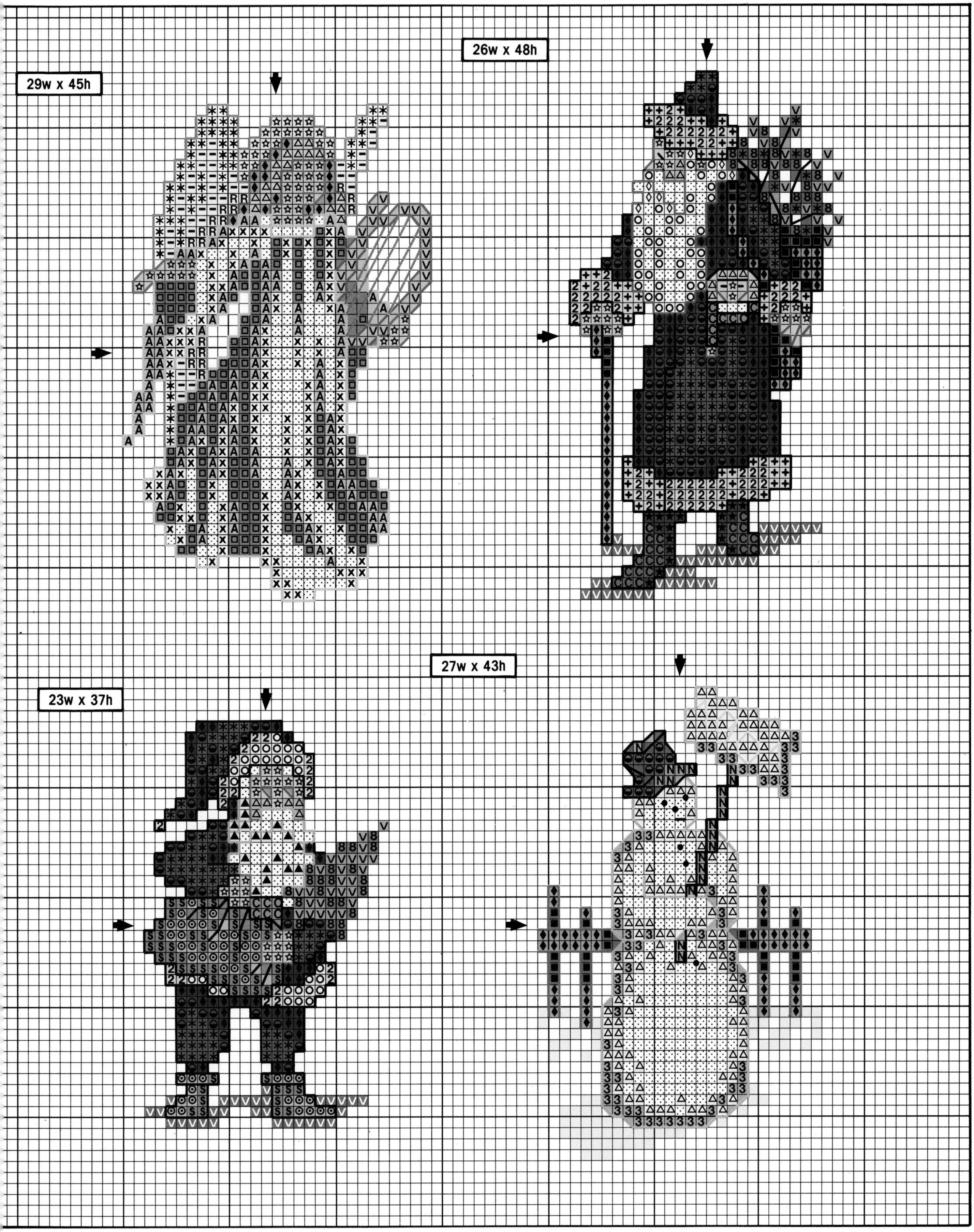
29w x 45h
26w x 48h
23w x 37h
27w x 43h

Liberty Angel

Liberty Angel (shown on page 39) was stitched over 2 fabric threads on a 16" x 22" piece of Cream Lugana (25 ct). Three strands of floss were used for Cross Stitch and 1 strand for Backstitch. It was made into a wall hanging.

For wall hanging, trim stitched piece 2½" larger than design on all sides.

For red fabric border, cut two 1¾"w x 18¼"l red fabric strips and two 1¾"w x 13¼"l red fabric strips. Matching right sides and raw edges, use a ½" seam allowance to sew one 18¼" strip to each side of stitched piece; press. Matching right sides and raw edges, use a ½" seam allowance to sew 13¼" strips to top and bottom edges of stitched piece; press.

For blue polka dot fabric border, cut two 2¼"w x 20"l blue polka dot fabric strips and two 2¼"w x 15½"l blue polka dot fabric strips. Matching right sides and raw edges, use a ½" seam allowance to sew one 20" blue polka dot strip to each side of red fabric border; press. Matching right sides and raw edges, use a ½" seam allowance to sew 15½" blue polka dot fabric strips to top and bottom of red fabric border; press.

For backing, cut a piece of fabric same size as wall hanging front. Cut a piece of low-loft polyester batting same size as backing fabric. Matching right sides and raw edges, place backing fabric on wall hanging front; place batting on backing fabric. Pin layers together.

Beginning at bottom edge and leaving an opening for turning, use a ½" seam allowance to sew layers together. Trim corners diagonally and turn right side out, carefully pushing corners outward. Whipstitch opening closed.

For hanging sleeve, cut a 3" x 14½" piece of fabric. Press edges ¼" to wrong side; press edges ¼" to wrong side again. Machine stitch pressed edges in place. With one long edge of hanging sleeve just below top edge of backing, center and pin hanging sleeve to wall hanging backing. Whipstitch long edges of hanging sleeve to backing; insert brass horn into hanging sleeve.

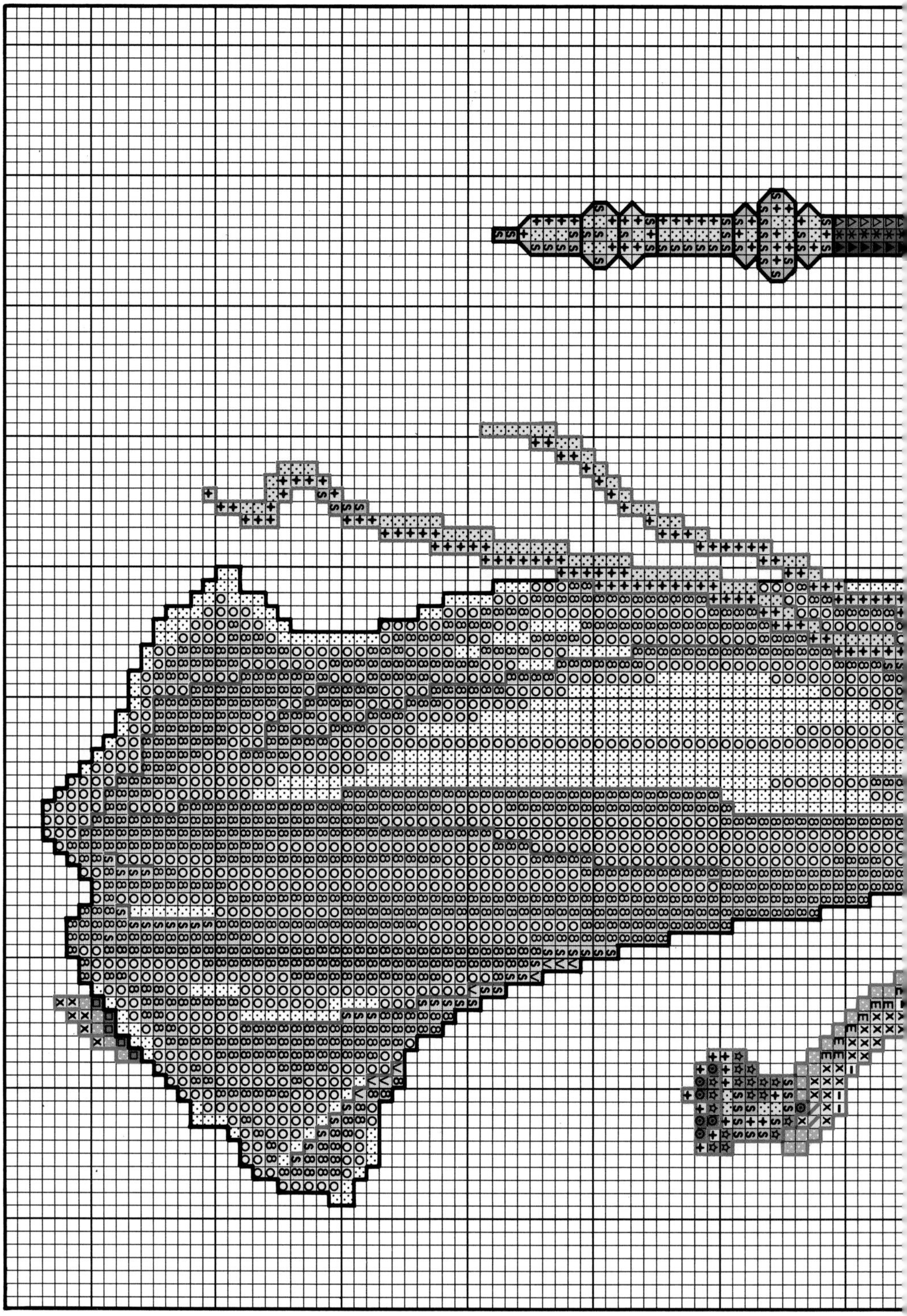

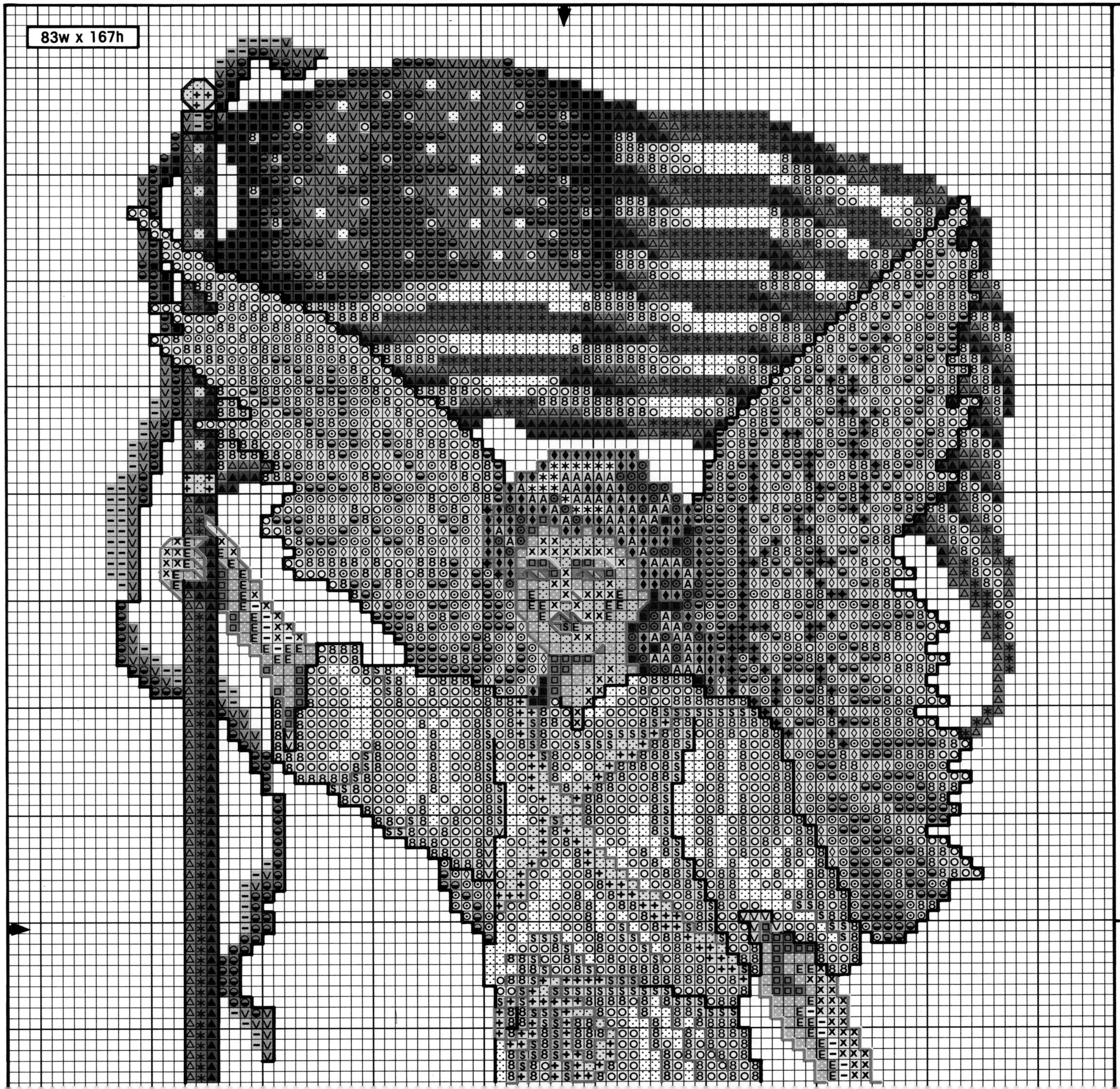

X	DMC	¼X	¾X	B'ST
⁙	blanc			
O	ecru			
✱	321			
E	353	◪		
	356			/
	433			/
◎	434			
♦	436			
A	437			
△	498	◪		
	640			/
V	642			
S	644			
⁙	725	◪		
✱	738			
X	754	◪		
⁙	758	◪		
S	760		◪	/
☆	781			
S	782	◪		
+	783	◪		
■	801	◪		
-	813			
▲	815	◪		
8	822			
■	824			
◒	825			
V	826			
	838			/
	930	◪		
-	951			
◊	3022	◪		
◎	3023			
◒	3024			
□	3064	◪		
	3371			/
⁙	3779	◪		
✦	3787			

□ Blue area indicates last row of top section of design.

58w x 79h
61w x 64h

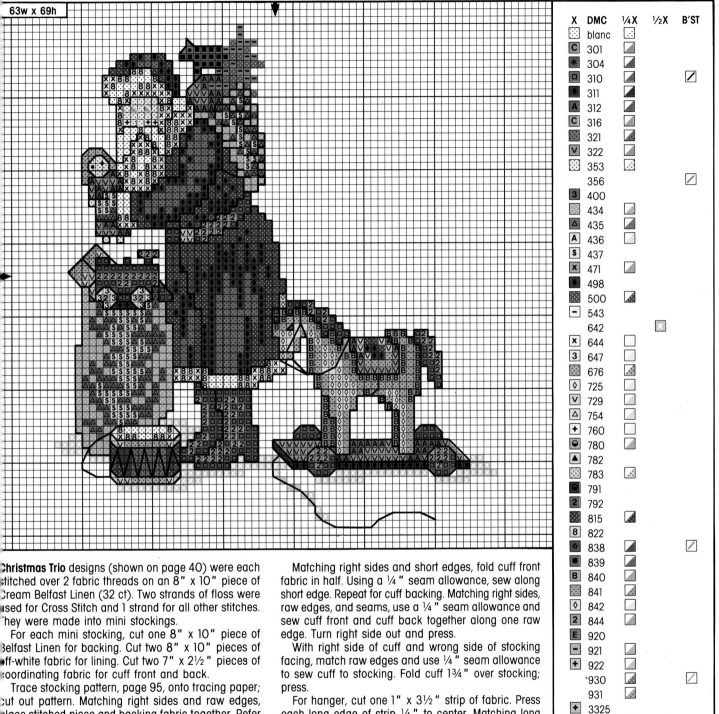

X	DMC	¼X	½X	B'ST
⁘	blanc	◩		
C	301	◩		
*	304	◩		
◘	310	◩		/
♦	311	◩		
A	312	◩		
C	316	◩		
⁘	321	◩		
V	322	◩		
⁘	353	◩		
	356			/
3	400			
⁘	434	◩		
△	435	◩		
A	436	◩		
S	437			
x	471	◩		
♦	498			
⁘	500	◩		
-	543			
	642		◩	
x	644	◩		
3	647	◩		
⁘	676	◩		
◊	725	◩		
V	729	◩		
△	754	◩		
+	760	◩		
◒	780	◩		
▲	782			
⁘	783	◩		
●	791			
2	792			
⁘	815	◩		
8	822			
☆	838	◩		/
■	839	◩		
B	840	◩		
⁘	841	◩		
◊	842	◩		
2	844	◩		
E	920			
-	921	◩		
+	922	◩		
	’930	◩		/
	931	◩		
+	3325			
◎	3345	◩		
-	3347			
	3371			/
★	3726	◩		
O	3727	◩		
☆	gold metallic	◩		/*
•	310 French Knot			
•	838 French Knot			

* Work in long stitches.

Christmas Trio designs (shown on page 40) were each stitched over 2 fabric threads on an 8" x 10" piece of Cream Belfast Linen (32 ct). Two strands of floss were used for Cross Stitch and 1 strand for all other stitches. They were made into mini stockings.

For each mini stocking, cut one 8" x 10" piece of Belfast Linen for backing. Cut two 8" x 10" pieces of off-white fabric for lining. Cut two 7" x 2½" pieces of coordinating fabric for cuff front and back.

Trace stocking pattern, page 95, onto tracing paper; cut out pattern. Matching right sides and raw edges, place stitched piece and backing fabric together. Refer to photo to position pattern on wrong side of stitched piece; pin pattern in place. Use fabric marking pencil to draw around pattern.

Leaving top edge open, sew stocking pieces together directly on drawn line. Trim seam allowance to ¼" and clip curves. Trim top edge along drawn line. Turn stocking right side out.

Repeat to draw around pattern and sew lining pieces together just inside drawn line. Trim seam allowance close to stitching. **Do not turn lining right side out.** Press top edge of lining ¼" to wrong side.

Matching right sides and short edges, fold cuff front fabric in half. Using a ¼" seam allowance, sew along short edge. Repeat for cuff backing. Matching right sides, raw edges, and seams, use a ¼" seam allowance and sew cuff front and cuff back together along one raw edge. Turn right side out and press.

With right side of cuff and wrong side of stocking facing, match raw edges and use ¼" seam allowance to sew cuff to stocking. Fold cuff 1¾" over stocking; press.

For hanger, cut one 1" x 3½" strip of fabric. Press each long edge of strip ¼" to center. Matching long edges, fold strip in half and sew close to folded edges. Matching short edges, fold hanger in half and whipstitch to inside of stocking at left seam.

With wrong sides facing, place lining inside stocking. Matching pressed edge of lining to seam of cuff, whipstitch lining to stocking.

the newborn king

X	DMC	¼X	½X	B'ST
⁙	blanc	◢		
○	ecru	◢		
□	309	◢		
◒	326	◢		
◊	335	◢		/
⊙	353	◢		
	355			/
■	500			
◆	501			
8	502			

X	DMC	¼X	½X	B'ST
C	503			
+	504			
▲	610	◢	S	/
✱	611	◢		
S	612	◢		
−	613			
■	640	◢		
◒	642	◢		
⁙	644	◢		
3	676	◢		

X	DMC	¼X	½X	B'ST
⁙	677	◢		
★	680	◢	V	
R	729	◢		
⁙	754	◢		
◒	758	◢		
C	760	◢		
■	815	◢		
✱	816	◢		
☆	822	◢		
⁙	899	◢		

X	DMC	¼X	½X	B'ST
■	930			
▲	931			
◒	932	◢		
A	963			
◆	3031	◢	X	
◆	3064	◢		
△	3326			
4	3371	◢		/
⁙	3750	◢		
S	3752	◢		

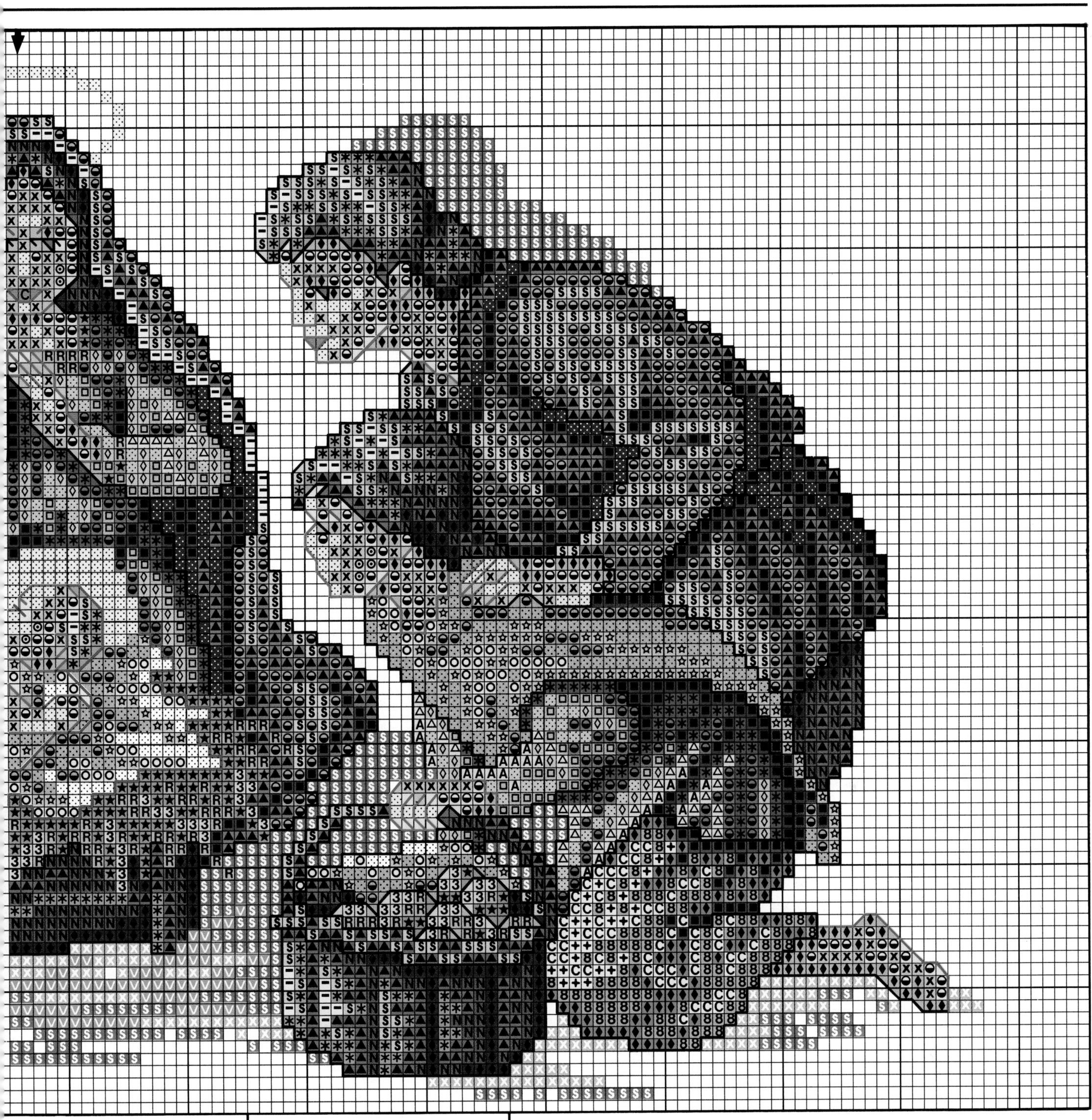

X	DMC	¼X	½X	B'ST
–	3753			
x	3779		◩	
N	3781		◩	
	Blue area indicates last row of right section of design.			

STITCH COUNT (162w x 85h)

Aida 11	14¾"	x	7¾"
Aida 14	11⅝"	x	6⅛"
Linen 32 over 2	10⅛"	x	5⅜"
Aida 18	9"	x	4¾"
Hardanger 22	7⅜"	x	3⅞"

The Newborn King (shown on page 42) was stitched over 2 fabric threads on a 19" x 14" piece of Raw Belfast Linen (32 ct). Two strands of floss were used for Cross Stitch and 1 strand for all other stitches. It was custom framed.

angels on high

DMC	¼X	B'ST
blanc	✓	
224		
225		
353		
356		✓
433	✓	✓
434	✓	
435	✓	
436		
437		

DMC	¼X	B'ST
640		
642	✓	
644		
754	✓	
758	✓	
760	✓	✓
822	✓	
927		
928		
931	✓	

DMC	¼X	B'ST
3021		✓
3022		
3023	✓	
3024	✓	
3064	✓	
3779	✓	
3787		✓

Pink area indicates last row of top section of design.

STITCH COUNT (118w x 152h)

Aida 11	10¾"	x	13⅞"
Aida 14	8½"	x	10⅞"
Linen 32 over 2	7⅜"	x	9½"
Aida 18	6⅝"	x	8½"
Hardanger 22	5⅜"	x	7"

Angels on High (shown on page 45) was stitched over 2 fabric threads on a 16" x 18" piece of White Belfast Linen (32 ct). Two strands of floss were used for Cross Stitch and 1 strand for Backstitch. It was custom framed.

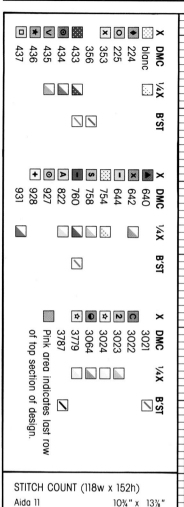

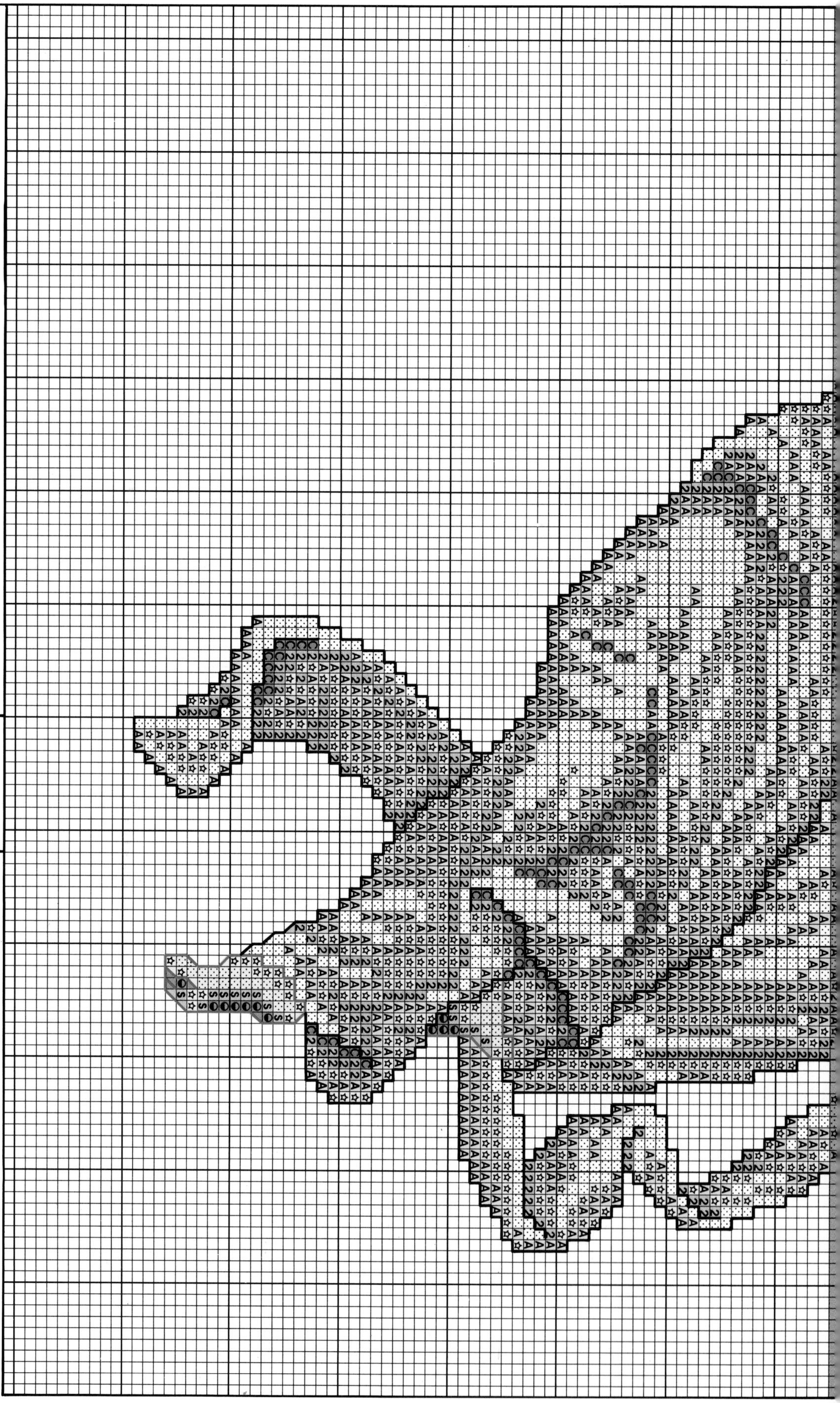

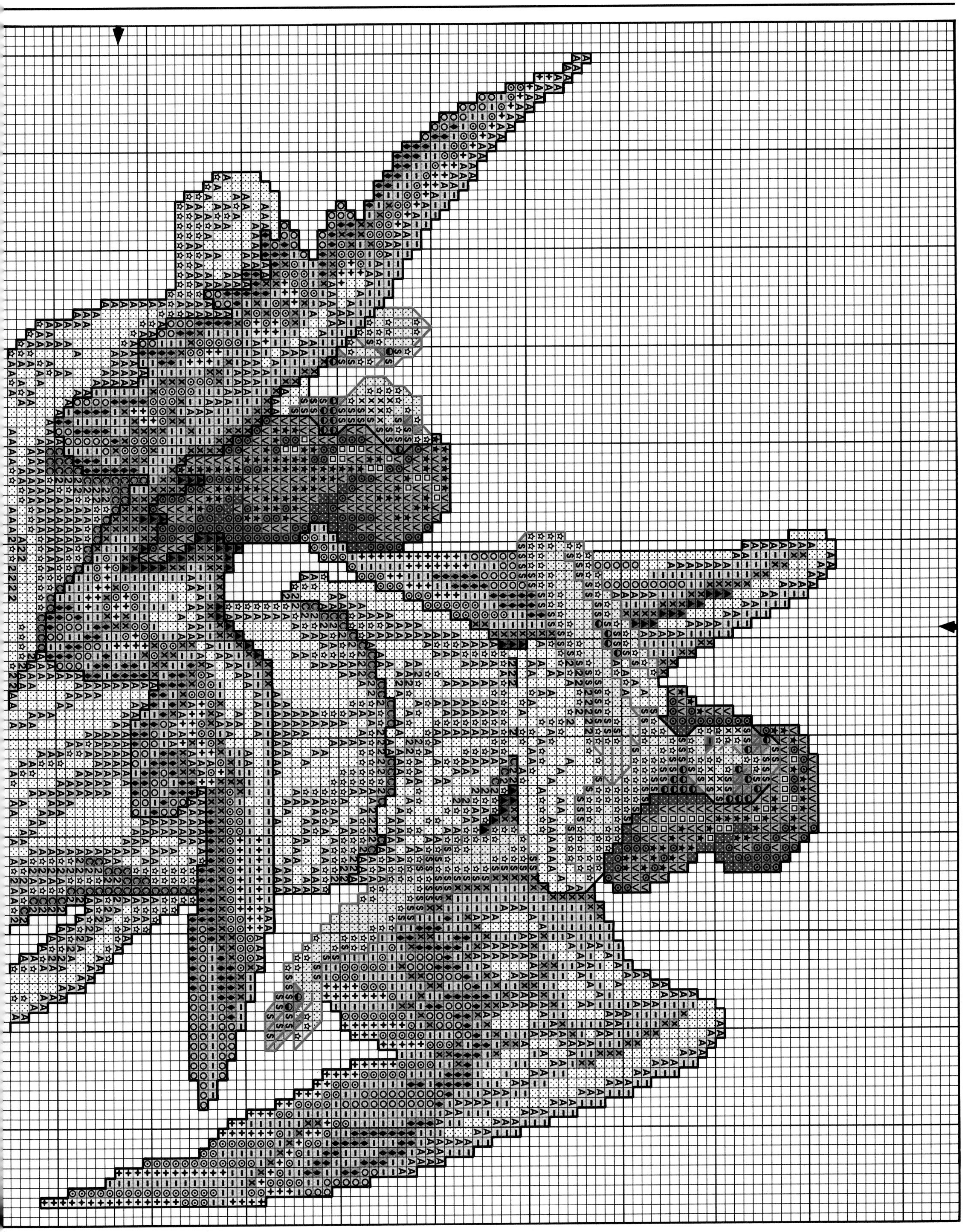

snow babies at play

Shown on page 46

Afghan: Designs were stitched over 2 fabric threads on a 45" x 58" piece of Taupe Anne Cloth (18 ct).

For afghan, cut off selvages of fabric; measure 5½" from raw edge of fabric and pull out 1 fabric thread. Fringe fabric up to missing fabric thread. Repeat for each side. Tie an overhand knot at each corner with 4 horizontal and 4 vertical threads. Working from corners, use 8 fabric threads for each knot until all threads are knotted.

Refer to Diagram for placement of designs on fabric; use 6 strands of floss for Cross Stitch and 2 strands for all other stitches.

Pillow: Design #3 was stitched over 2 fabric threads on an 11" pillow square of Taupe Anne Cloth (18 ct). Six strands of floss were used for Cross Stitch and 2 strands for all other stitches.

For pillow, use same color 11" pillow square for backing. Matching wrong sides and raw edges, place stitched piece and backing fabric together. Leaving an opening for stuffing, sew around fabric 1¼" from outer raised threads. Stuff pillow with polyester fiberfill and sew opening closed. Fringe fabric to machine-stitched lines.

Fringed Ornaments: Designs #2 and #6 were each stitched over 2 fabric threads on a 7" square of Raw Belfast Linen (32 ct). Two strands of floss were used for Cross Stitch and 1 strand for all other stitches.

For each ornament, trim stitched piece 1" larger than design on all sides. Cut one piece of Belfast Linen same size as stitched piece for backing. With wrong sides facing, use ecru floss to Cross Stitch fabric pieces together ½" from sides and bottom. Stuff with polyester fiberfill.

For hanger, fold a 6" length of ⅛"w ribbon in half; place ends of ribbon between fabric pieces in center of top edge. Catching ribbon ends in stitching, cross stitch across top of ornament ½" from edge. Fringe fabric to cross-stitched lines.

Diagram

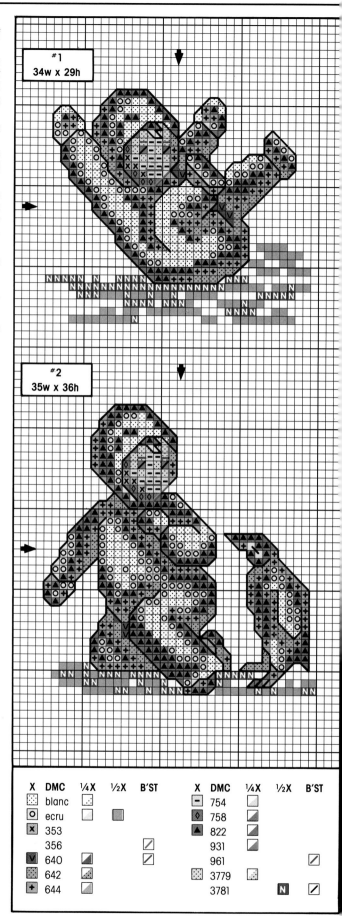

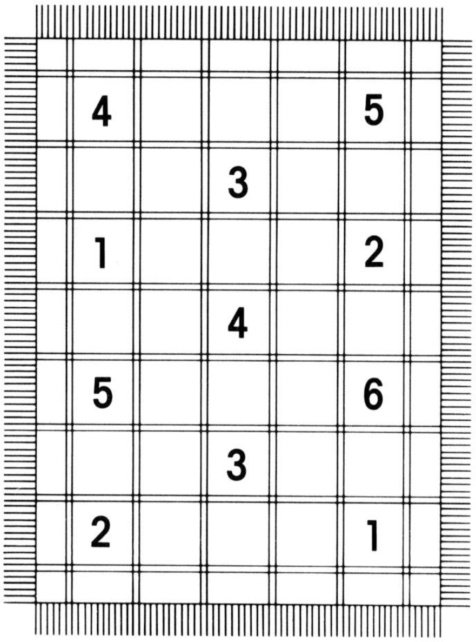

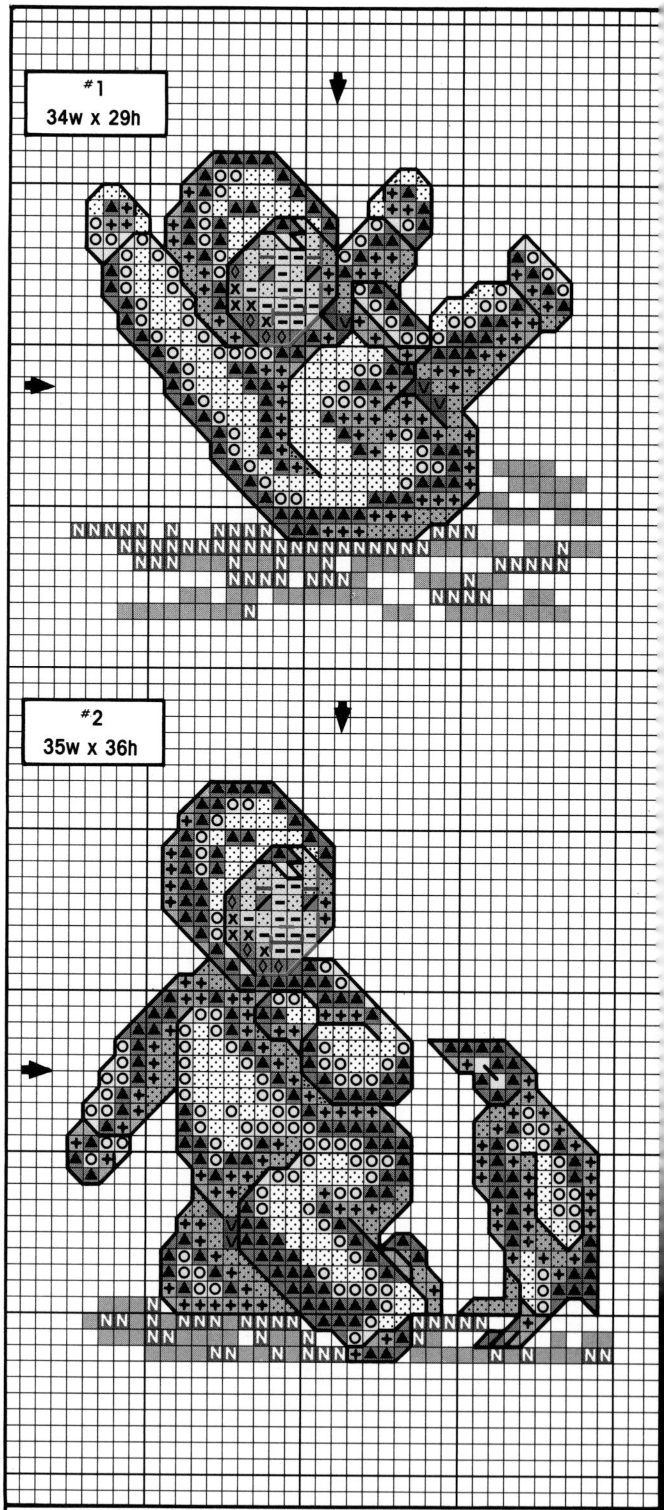

X	DMC	¼X	½X	B'ST
⁘	blanc	⁘		
O	ecru	▫	■	
X	353			
	356			/
V	640	◢		/
⁘	642	◢		
+	644	◢		
–	754	◢		
◊	758	◢		
▲	822	◢		
	931	◢		
	961			/
⁘	3779	⁘		
	3781		N	/

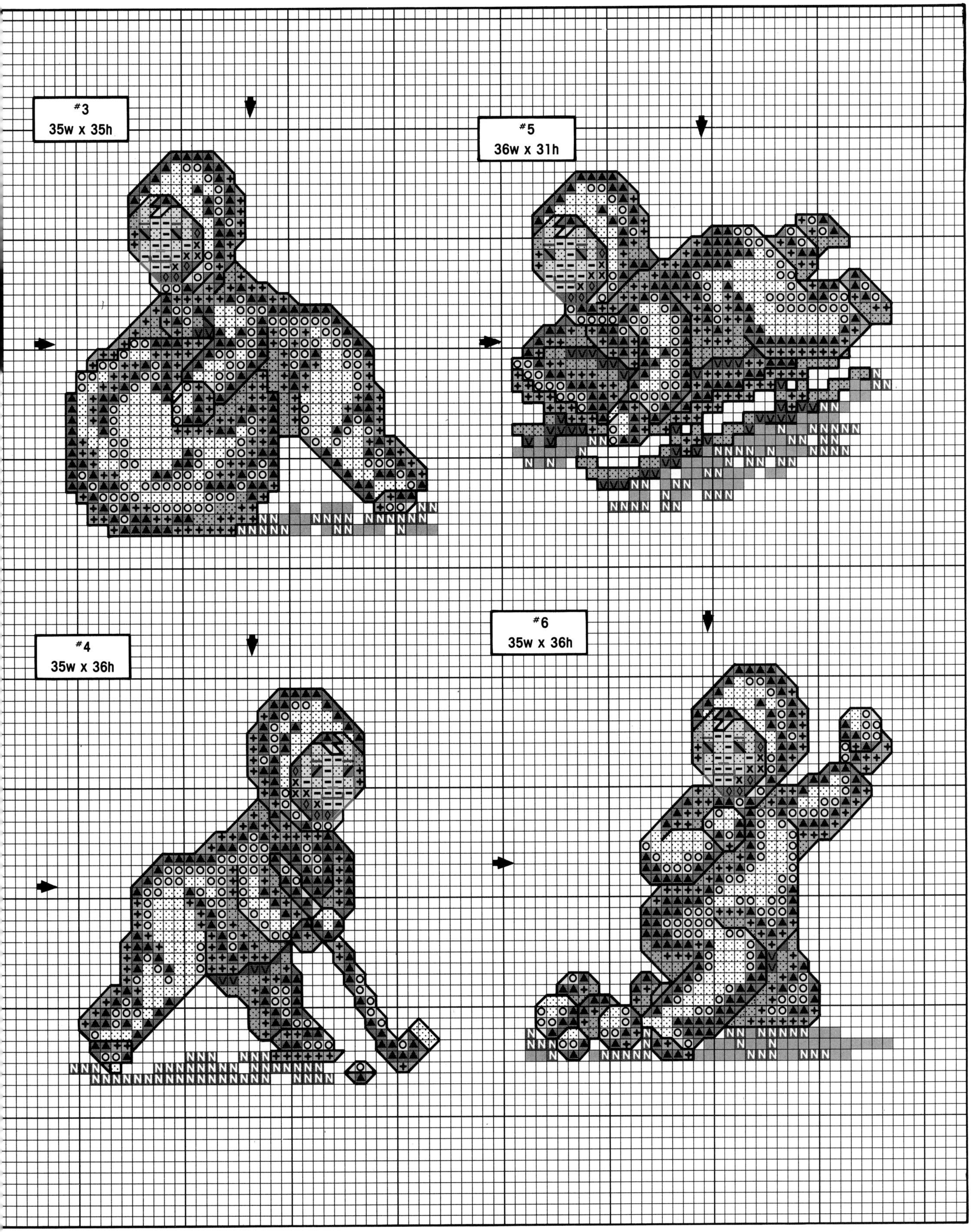
#3
35w x 35h
#5
36w x 31h
#4
35w x 36h
#6
35w x 36h

christkindl

X	DMC	¼X	¾X	½X	B'ST
	blanc	■			
O	ecru	■			
	221				■
2	223	■			
	224	■			
–	353	■			
	356				■
A	420	■			
x	597	■			
	598	■			
◎	676	■			
△	677	■		■	
S	680	■			
	729	■			■
	754	■	■		
x	758	■			
	806	■			
	807	■			
	869				■
	961				■
■	3031	■			■
▲	3032	■			
V	3033	■			
★	3064	■			
E	3328	■			
♦	3345	■			
◎	3346	■			
x	3347	■			
C	3712	■			
♦	3721	■			
◒	3722	■			
	3765				■
□	3779	■			
★	3781	■			
✱	3782	■			
	3790	■		■	

hristkindl designs (shown on page 49) were each stitched on an 8" quare of Ivory Hardanger (22 ct). One strand of floss was used for all itches. They were made into stuffed ornaments.

For each stuffed ornament, cut one 8" square of Hardanger for backing. ace desired pattern onto tracing paper; cut out pattern. Matching right des and raw edges, place stitched piece and backing fabric together. efer to photo to position pattern on wrong side of stitched piece; pin attern in place. Use fabric marking pencil to draw around pattern. Leaving an opening for turning, sew fabric pieces together directly on drawn line. Leaving a ¼" seam allowance, cut out ornament. Clip seam allowance at curves and corners. Turn ornament right side out, carefully pushing corners outward. Stuff ornament with polyester fiberfill and sew final closure by hand. Using nylon line, whipstitch gold metallic cord to ornament along seamline.

For hanger, run a 10" length of nylon line through backing fabric at top center of ornament; knot ends together.

GENERAL INSTRUCTIONS

WORKING WITH CHARTS

How to Read Charts: Each of the designs is shown in chart form. Each colored square on the charts represents one Cross Stitch or one Half Cross Stitch. Black or colored dots represent French Knots. The straight lines on the charts indicate Backstitch. When a French Knot or a Backstitch crosses the square, the symbol is omitted.

Each chart is accompanied by a color key. This key indicates the color of floss to use for each stitch on the chart. The headings on the color key are for Cross Stitch (**X**), DMC color number (**DMC**), Quarter Stitch (**¼X**), Three-Quarter Stitch (**¾X**), Half Cross Stitch (**½X**), and Backstitch (**B'ST**). Color key columns should be read vertically and horizontally to determine type of stitch and floss color.

Where to Start: The horizontal and vertical centers of each charted design are shown by arrows. You may start at any point on the charted design, but be sure the design will be centered on the fabric. Locate the center of fabric by folding in half, top to bottom and again left to right. On the charted design, count the number of squares (stitches) from the center of the chart to where you wish to start. Then from the fabric's center, find your starting point by counting out the same number of fabric threads (stitches). (**Note:** To work over two fabric threads, count out twice the number of fabric threads.)

STITCH DIAGRAMS

Counted Cross Stitch (X): Work one Cross Stitch to correspond to each colored square on the chart. For horizontal rows, work stitches in two journeys (**Fig. 1**). For vertical rows, complete each stitch as shown (**Fig. 2**). When working over 2 fabric threads, work Cross Stitch as shown in **Fig. 3**. When the chart shows a Backstitch crossing a colored square (**Fig. 4**), a Cross Stitch should be worked first; then the Backstitch should be worked on top of the Cross Stitch.

Fig. 1

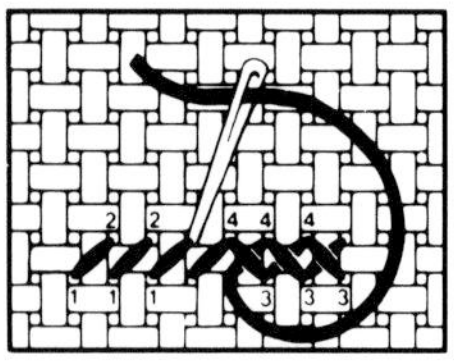

Fig. 2

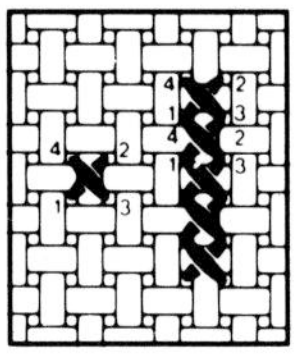

Fig. 3

Fig. 4

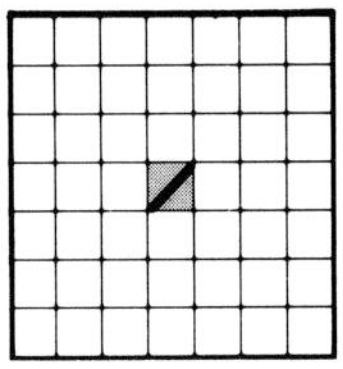

Quarter Stitch (¼X and ¾X): Quarter Stitches are denoted by triangular shapes of color on the chart and on the color key. Come up at 1 (**Fig. 5**); then split fabric thread to go down at 2. When stitches 1-4 are worked in the same color, the resulting stitch is called a Three-Quarter Stitch (¾X). **Fig. 6** shows the technique for Quarter Stitches when working over 2 fabric threads.

Fig. 5

Fig. 6

Half Cross Stitch (½X): This stitch is one journey of the Cross Stitch and is worked from lower left to upper right. **Fig. 7** shows the Half Cross Stitch worked over 2 fabric threads.

Fig. 7

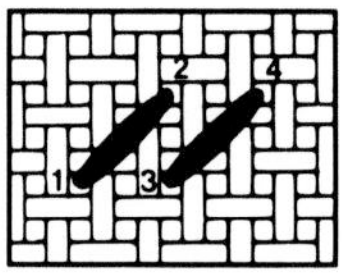

Backstitch (B'ST): For outline detail, Backstitch (shown on chart and on color key by black or colored straight lines) should be worked after the design has been completed (**Fig. 8**).

Fig. 8

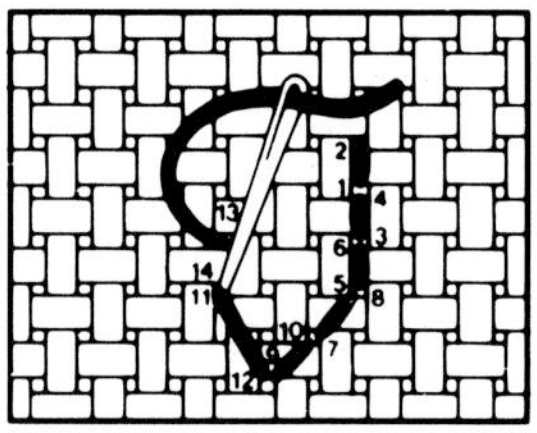

French Knot: Bring needle up at 1. Wrap floss once around needle and insert needle at 2, holding end of floss with non-stitching fingers (**Fig. 9**). Tighten knot; then pull needle through fabric, holding floss until it must be released. For larger knot, use more strands; wrap only once.

Fig. 9

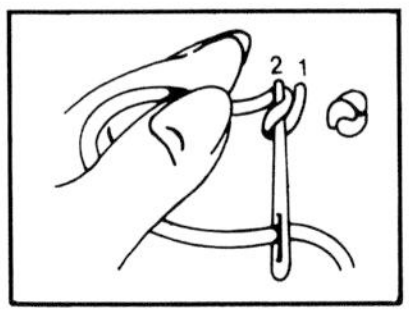

STITCHING TIPS

Working Over Two Fabric Threads: Using a hoo is optional when working over two fabr threads. To work without a hoop, roll the exces fabric from left to right until working area in the proper position. Using the sewin method instead of the stab method, wo stitches over two fabric threads on the fro of the fabric. To add support to the stitche it is important that the first Cross Stitch placed on the fabric with stitch 1-2 beginnin and ending where a vertical fabric threa crosses over a horizontal fabric threa (**Fig. 10**). When the first stitch is in the corre position, the entire design will be place properly, with vertical fabric threads supportin each stitch.

Fig. 10

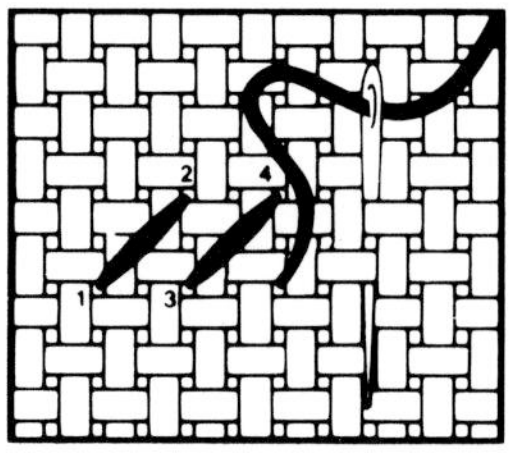

Working on Waste Canvas: Waste canvas is special canvas that provides an evenweav grid for placing stitches on fabric. After th design is worked over the canvas, the canva threads are removed, leaving the design on th fabric. The canvas is available in several mes sizes.

1. Cover edges of canvas with masking tap Cut a piece of lightweight non-fusib interfacing the same size as canvas to provid a firm stitching base.

2. Find desired stitching area on fabric ar mark center of area with a pin. Match cent of canvas to pin on fabric. Pin canvas to fabri pin interfacing to wrong side. Baste all thre thicknesses together.

3. Using a sharp needle, work design, stitchin from large holes to large holes.

4. Trim canvas to within ¾" of desig Dampen canvas until it becomes limp. Pull o canvas threads one at a time using tweezer

5. Trim interfacing close to design.

Diagram

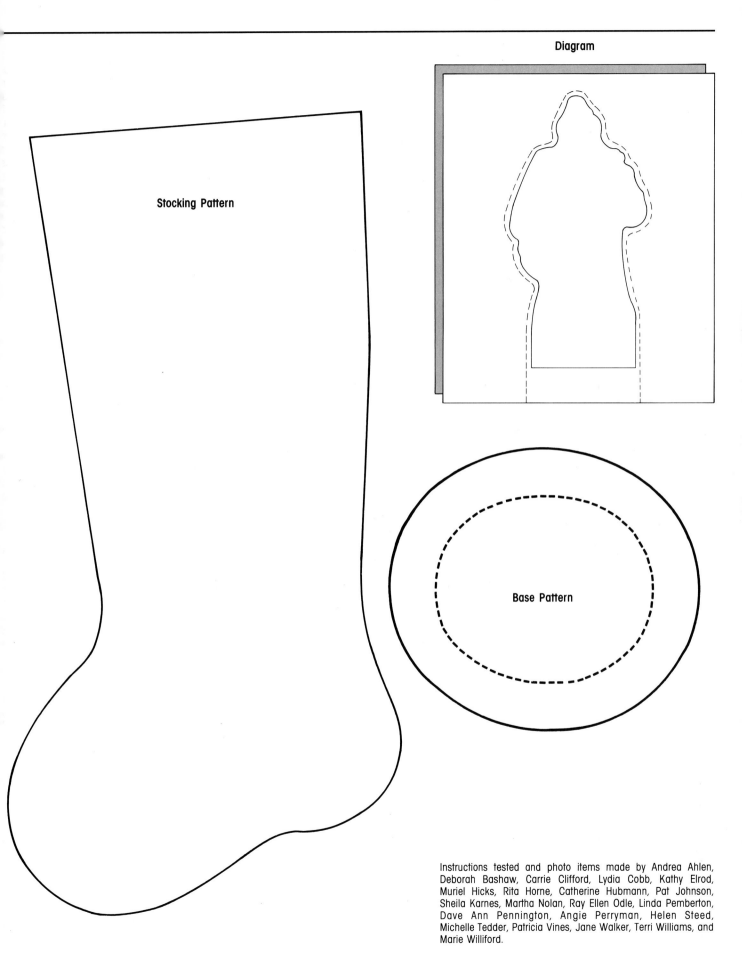

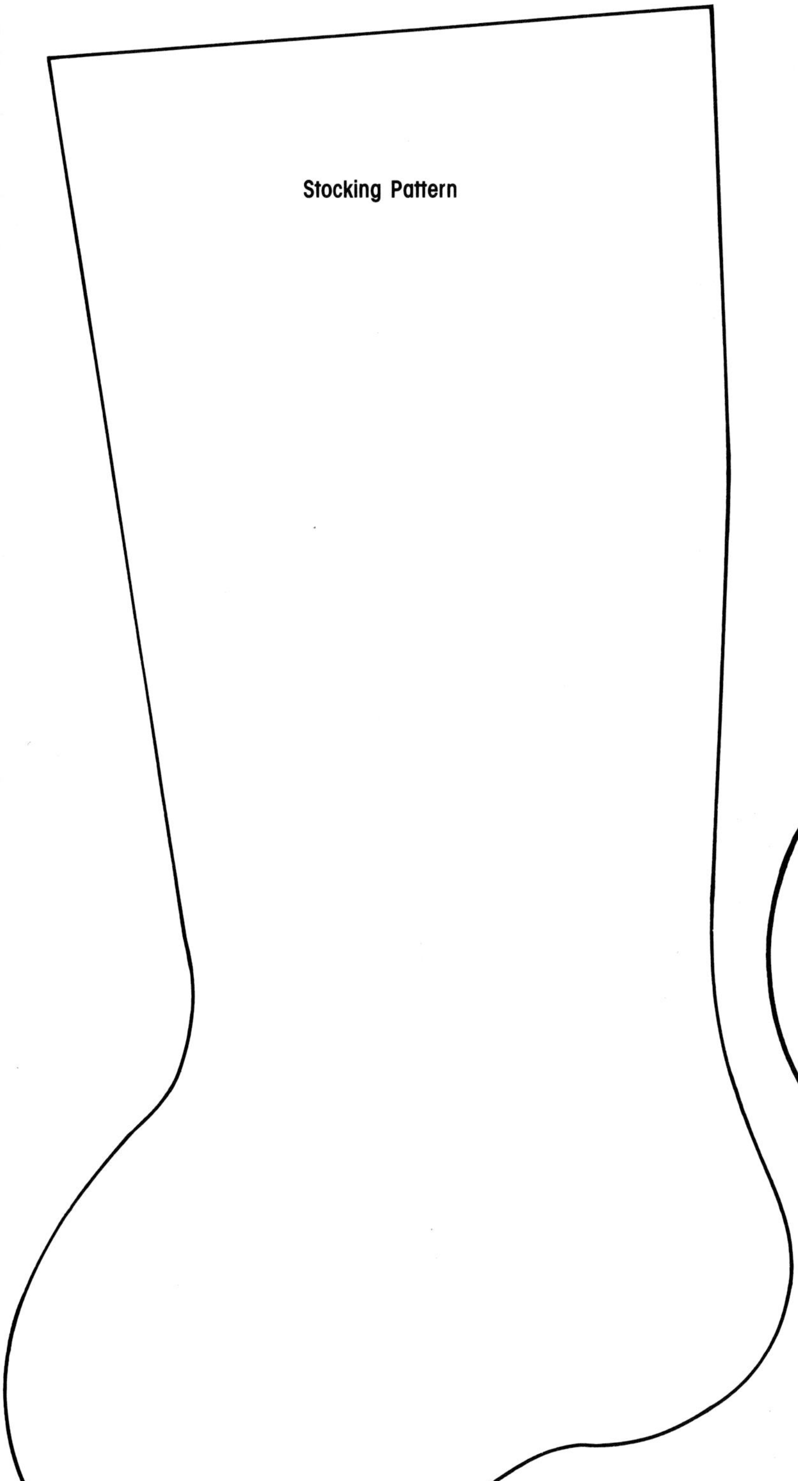

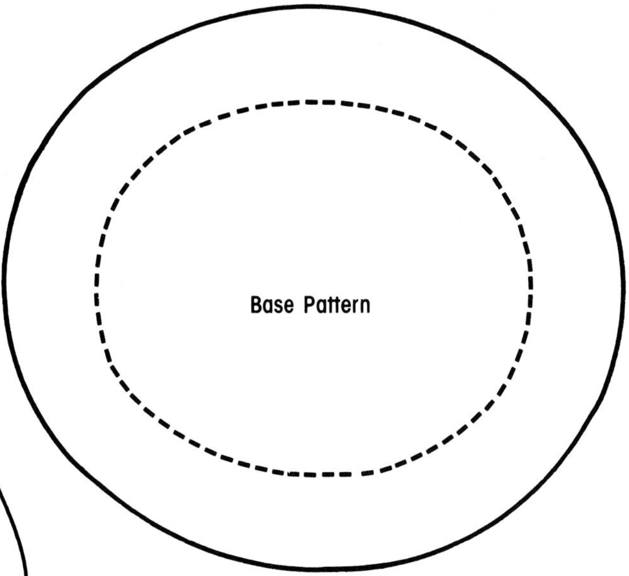

Instructions tested and photo items made by Andrea Ahlen, Deborah Bashaw, Carrie Clifford, Lydia Cobb, Kathy Elrod, Muriel Hicks, Rita Horne, Catherine Hubmann, Pat Johnson, Sheila Karnes, Martha Nolan, Ray Ellen Odle, Linda Pemberton, Dave Ann Pennington, Angie Perryman, Helen Steed, Michelle Tedder, Patricia Vines, Jane Walker, Terri Williams, and Marie Williford.

CHRISTMAS
LIGHTS

FELIZ
NAVIDAD

Christmas
GIFTS
OF GOOD TASTE